Rider's
Complete Guide To
Motorcycle
Touring

Rider's
Complete Guide To
Motorcycle Touring

By Dick Blom and the Editors of Rider Magazine

Editor in Charge: Patrick J. Flaherty

Published by TL Enterprises, Inc.
29901 Agoura Rd., Agoura, California 91301

Book Division
TL Enterprises, Inc.

Art Rouse
Chairman of the Board

Richard Rouse
President

Denis Rouse
Executive Vice President/Publisher

Patrick J. Flaherty
Vice President/Editor-In-Chief

Bill Estes
Vice President/Technical Editor

Dana Brown
Vice President/Production Director

Composition By:
Publisher's Typography
(A Division of TL Enterprises, Inc.)
Book Design: Bob Schroeder
Illustrator: Gary McAllister
Associate Editor: Pamela Taylor
Editorial Assistants: Tina Hill,
    Pat Kolb

Foreword

I've been a motorcycle enthusiast ever since I've been old enough to have a driver's license. But the touring bug didn't really bite me until a couple of years ago. If only *I* could have had a book like this when I was just starting out!

I realize, of course, that this volume has been preceded by other books on the subject. But for the most part, they've been only marginally useful to enthusiasts looking for solid, up-to-date, how-to-do-it information.

Here, at last, is a book that delivers exactly that. And it's written, with the able assistance of the editors of *Rider* magazine, by perhaps the most well-traveled and thoroughly knowledgeable rider on the road, *Rider's* own Dick Blom.

That Dick is uniquely qualified to write this book—the result of more than 30 years and hundreds of thousands of miles of road riding experience—will be evident to you after the first few pages. For here, in Dick's friendly but unmistakably authoritative style, is literally *everything* you need to know to make your two wheel adventures more enjoyable, comfortable and safer than ever before.

Whether you're a green beginner or an avid veteran cycle traveler, I guarantee that you will benefit tremendously from the wealth of invaluable road-proven experience and expert advice you'll find between these covers.

After all, doing it right is a big part of the fun. So please read and enjoy what will undoubtedly be *the* motorcycle touring textbook for years to come.

Denis Rouse
Publisher

Contents

Chapter 1
Why Go Touring?

Most of us start riding a motorcycle because it is faster than a bicycle and cheaper than a car. We use it for awhile as our main form of transportation and soon realize that it is much better than having to wait for a bus; that it beats the uncertainty of hitchhiking when traveling farther afield.

Sunshine and motorcycles are an attractive combination and it is not surprising that most first-time riders start out in good weather. By the time we've learned how to ride and the weather has turned bad, it's too late—we're hooked.

It's funny the way it happens. At first, it is a practical way to get about, the only thing we can afford. Next thing we know, we are going off for a ride just because it seems like a good idea to be riding. All of a sudden we realize, it's crazy, but we actually like it.

I think I may have been slower than most in realizing I'd been caught. The revelation came to me at a most unusual time. I was out in a really nasty rainstorm and since there was no place suitable to stop for shelter, I decided to keep on riding. It was summer and quite warm, so I felt sure it would not be too bad.

I was wrong. That has to have been one of the coldest, most miserable rides of my life. It rained so hard that by the end of the journey the water was actually running *out* of my boots.

So did I decide right then and there to quit motorcycling and get myself a car, which by then I could have afforded? No way. My reaction was to find myself some proper clothing, so I could ride more comfortably in rain like I'd just encountered. That has been my attitude toward bad weather motorcycling ever since. You don't stop riding; you just figure out what you need to make it possible and more enjoyable.

For several more years I rode, quite happy in the knowledge that I did so because I enjoyed it. Then one day a horrible thought struck me. What on earth was it that attracted me to motorcycling? Was there something wrong with me that I enjoyed it so much? I consider myself a reasonably well-educated, thinking person and for a short time it bothered me that something that was simply "fun" should have such a hold on me and should be so much a part of my life. I tried to analyze what it was that appealed

A deep-seated love of freedom, a thirst for travel and adventure, a need to express his individuality—such are the bonds that link the lone cowboy of yesteryear with the motorcycle rider of today.

to me about motorcycling. Did I really need the excitement, the exposure to danger, the thrills and pleasure that it offered? Since that was almost 30 years ago, and I'm still riding, it seems that I did. In fact, as I have discovered more of the benefits of motorcycles, my addiction to them has grown.

When a fascination with travel is combined with this love of motorcycling, touring seems like the logical answer. Many people harbor a desire to "see the other side of the mountain" at some point in their lives, and motorcyclists have a better opportunity than most of fulfilling this ambition. As Americans, our heritage is heavily laced with the spirit of adventure, passed down to us by explorers of the new country. From an early age we thrilled to tales of the lone trapper who suffered and struggled in his search for pelts, motivated more by his love for freedom than for money. He faced the wilderness on its own terms and lived or died by his ability to meet its requirements.

Among our childhood heroes was the lone cowboy riding the western plains, just a drifter, a wanderer, his horse his only true friend and his only possessions—just some clothes and a bedroll—lashed behind his saddle. No doubt this romantic character is much greater in fiction than in fact, but he captures the imagination and is a popular figure of our folklore.

Consider now the modern-day motorcycle rider traveling the unknown road, his machine heavily laden with camping gear. Perhaps he is not as far removed from those early explorers and settlers as we might imagine. Perhaps this, in part, explains the lure of motorcycle travel for so many riders, for it offers a chance to explore new territory and to tackle the elements—an opportunity for real adventure.

Any long trip, however dull its destination, becomes something worth looking forward to if you are going by motorcycle. In the same way, a week or two away on the bike can transform a normally pleasant vacation trip into one of life's unforgettable experiences.

It eventually dawned on me that I actually enjoyed being different—that I liked the individuality that my motorcycle gave me. Most touring riders are related to, work with, and live near non-motorcyclists and it is fun to shock them a bit by casually mentioning, "I think I'll ride to the West Coast this summer!" or some equally distant point. You'll get some response every time; sometimes negative, sometimes sheer awe and admiration, more often just pure disbelief! Only if you tour on a motorcycle will you know that any place in the United States, and beyond, is within reach if you really want it to be.

My motorcycle has become a "magic carpet" that can take me any place that there's a track or road. I first realized this when I was out one night putting some easy break-in miles on a brand new BMW. I had just traveled up the coast road, California's Highway 1, through Huntington Beach. It's an attractive route, running parallel to the beach almost all the way, and, since my bike was running perfectly, I was feeling rather good about the whole ride.

I turned off this road and started to head east. As I did, I experienced a vision that has stuck with me ever since, as clearly as if it happened yesterday. With the full expanse of the Pacific Ocean directly behind me, it suddenly seemed as if my motorcycle and I had grown enormously, at the same time as the whole of the United States had shrunk before us. As I rode slowly along, I could visualize the country laid out before me. Texas was off to the right, and, looking over it, I could just make out Florida and see the little causeway road leading down to Key West. Running my eye along the Rocky Mountains, I could see all the places I'd like to visit in the West—Yellowstone and Glacier National Parks, the mountains and valleys of Colorado, Wyoming and Montana and more, much more.

It was at that moment that I knew my motorcycle had great powers, that it could take me anywhere, that distances would no longer be a barrier, and that I was going to travel and travel until I'd seen everything I could ever want to see. I have no idea how long this strange experience lasted. I only know that it is as true for me today as it was then, and it pretty much describes how I feel about touring on a motorcycle.

Motorcycles have to be one of the best—and least expensive—ways to travel and see the country. Yet it is often difficult to sell the idea to people who only travel by car. They are constantly puzzled by my enthusiasm for motorcycle touring and, in a way, I can understand it. No doubt they are combining the boredom of traveling long distance in a car with the lack of apparent comfort on a motorcycle. It certainly does not sound very appealing. What they are missing is the difference between traveling cooped up in a car, watching everything through windows, and the incredible pleasure of being on a motorcycle, feeling so much a part of your surroundings. The rider is aware of almost everything around him, every new sight, sound and smell, while the car traveler is generally more aware of the music on his radio. It can best be likened to the difference between seeing a good football game on TV and going to the stadium to watch it, being able to enjoy the full impact of the colors, sounds and whole atmosphere, including the excitement of the crowd. You may not have actually seen more, but it was a total experience, one that will stay in your memory as something in which you took part, rather than just saw.

Road maps hold a fascination for me. I thoroughly enjoy browsing through them, planning routes which, at the time, I have little chance of taking but which somehow or other, I eventually travel.

Motorcycle touring is not just a matter of covering a lot of miles, although that's part of it. Far more significantly, it is a way of exploring the country and meeting new people; it is a chance to get out of your everyday skin and become completely involved in new experiences. I get a lot of pleasure from planning my tours. I really enjoy the preparation—selecting my routes, choosing the places I will visit and deciding what gear I ought to take along. It is extremely pleasing to be able to go through a series of weather changes while on the road, being properly equipped for each. There is something intensely satisfying about being all packed up and out on the road, heading off on an extended tour, your bike feeling light and responsive, yet knowing you have everything you need to travel and camp comfortably for days or weeks. It adds to the feeling of complete independence that one experiences when touring . . . the knowledge that you can respond to your every whim, follow whatever road looks inviting, stop where and when you feel like it and have all the essentials to be comfortable wherever you happen to be.

After a week or so on the road, I start to develop a feeling of detachment, of complete removal from home, work and friends. There is no thought of departure or return, just the road I'm riding and the countryside through which I'm passing. Each day merges with the next, with no clear yesterdays or tomorrows. The only thing that matters is the completely absorbing task of riding the bike.

Even riding becomes more enjoyable as the days slide by; my body and the machine seem to fit each other perfectly. After a few days or a week I am no longer aware of any aches or pains from riding the bike and only complete enjoyment is left. I become less and less aware of any discomfort from coldness or heat and more in tune with the sights, sounds and smells of my environment.

Part of the pleasure of traveling comes from just visiting the different parts of this vast and varied country, from observing the changing styles of architecture, farming methods and equipment, to seeing the wildlife and flora, tasting local foods and hearing other accents.

Touring gives you a lot of time to think. While one part of your mind is concentrating on riding and absorbing your changing surroundings, another part is able to roam free. You experience complete isolation, even when riding two-up, and this can lead to some serious reflection on your life—past, present and future. It gives you a chance to look at problems more objectively, and simply by "getting away from it all," things frequently just fall into place and solutions become obvious. It is not only a good time to get back in touch with yourself, but also a splendid way of meeting others and making new friends. It is worth taking the time to get to know people you meet on the road, finding out about their lives, beliefs and expectations. It can be a real eye-opener at times.

Your motorcycle offers you the chance to do this. The fact that it is packed for touring makes it—and you—objects of interest to both other riders and local residents. If you take the trouble to talk to locals, you may also pick up a lot of useful information, such as the location of good camping or fishing spots, or the date of some forthcoming festival or event that would be of interest to you.

Basically, only one qualification is needed to go touring and that's a love of motorcycle riding. This reminds me of the time I was riding across the Arizona desert at the end of a particularly lengthy tour. I was on a dull stretch of the interstate and it was a hot day. It did not make sense that I should be enjoying myself as much as I was. There I was, loving the slight coolness of the wind, feeling pleased with the way the bike was handling and running. I'd been away for several weeks and had been on the road for almost all that time. Yet I was still reluctant to be heading home.

It seems there is no end to touring. Once you've had a taste of being on the road, you are going to want more, and the more you travel, the better it's going to get.

Chapter 2
Getting Started

Once you have made up your mind to go touring, you will be faced with a whole range of questions to be answered and decisions to be made.

Will you go solo or two-up, traveling on your own or as one of a group? What kind of time will your schedule allow? How much attention should you pay to finances, and how can you economize? What aspect of touring most appeals to you? Is it the riding itself, the traveling, the total break with routine, the challenge of making long trips on a bike, or the chance to be outdoors for weeks at a time while you ride and camp your way around the country?

It is not critical to have all the answers right away, nor is it necessary to be absolutely sure what aspect of motorcycle touring interests you most, but it is worth giving it all some thought. It will help to narrow down the vast number of choices open to you and give you a chance to start selecting equipment and making preparations. Often, it will depend on your present attitude toward motorcycling, your riding ability and your bike, if you already own one. Is your machine suitable for touring, at least good enough to get you started? What riding experience do you have that will help you tackle a motorcycle tour? All these factors will help determine when and how you start out traveling long distances on the road.

One of the first things you will need to do is to select suitable equipment. Most important here is your choice of motorcycle, and we have devoted a whole chapter to this subject. There are, however, one or two points worth emphasizing here. It is all too easy to decide that your requirements are for a large touring bike, while forgetting that your riding skills may not be sufficient to make it a sensible choice, at least for the time being. Some of the large 1,000cc machines are incredibly fast and will out-accelerate any car on the road; the power is awesome. They are also surprisingly easy to ride, but that does not make them safe for inexperienced riders. It takes time to acquire the road sense and skills you need to be able to cope with a large capacity machine under any conditions, but unfortunately many riders choose to ignore this. The situation becomes even worse when the machine is loaded up with accessories and touring gear, for it then requires additional skill to be able to handle it well and ride

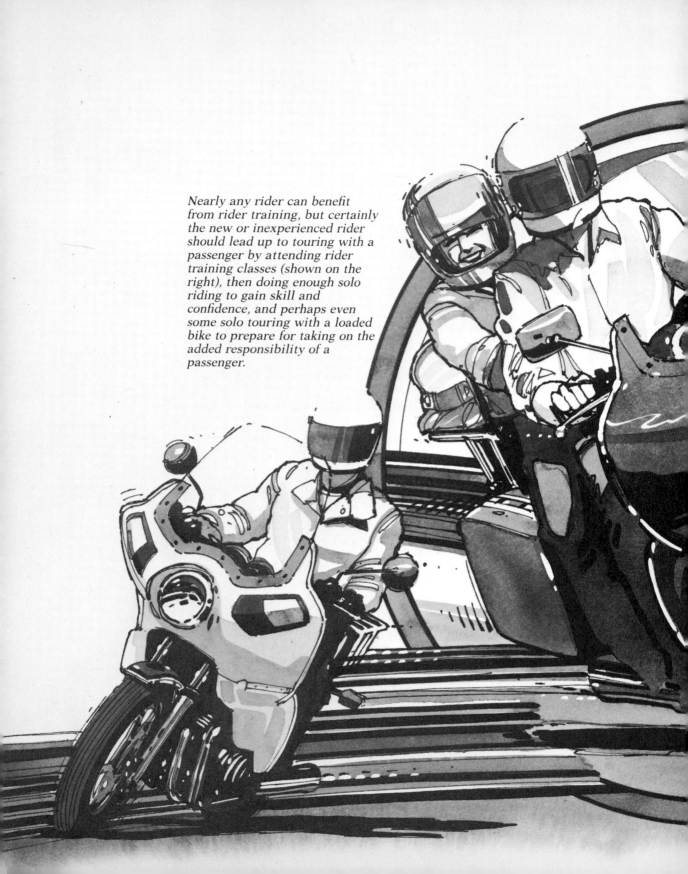

Nearly any rider can benefit from rider training, but certainly the new or inexperienced rider should lead up to touring with a passenger by attending rider training classes (shown on the right), then doing enough solo riding to gain skill and confidence, and perhaps even some solo touring with a loaded bike to prepare for taking on the added responsibility of a passenger.

it safely.

For example, it is all too easy for a big frame-mounted fairing to make you feel like you're traveling more slowly than you really are. Then there is the effect a load will have on stopping distances. Sometimes it can substantially increase them, but the inexperienced rider may be unaware of it since there is often little difference in the acceleration of the bike.

For anyone new to motorcycling, I would highly recommend a riding course. This type of course is now available in most parts of the country and, in many cases, it is not even essential that you own your own motorcycle, as loan bikes are oftentimes available for students' use. Courses are run by both public schools and private groups. The most common is the Motorcycle Rider Course, developed by the Motorcycle Safety Foundation. The MSF trains instructors and publishes most of the course material used by the schools that run these courses. If you wish to find out what courses are available in your area and who you should contact, the MSF office is located at 6755 Elkridge Landing Road, Linthicum, Maryland 21090. The phone number is (301) 768-3060.

Most of these classes are designed for the novice rider, but there are more advanced courses for riders with some experience. These classes have proved to be extremely worthwhile and consistently turn out better, safer riders.

Let us now consider the case of a completely new rider who wants to go motorcycle touring—possibly even someone who has never ridden a bike before, but perhaps got a taste for touring by traveling as a passenger. The first step should be to find the nearest Motorcycle Rider Course and enroll as soon as possible. Even if it feels strange at first to be riding a bike, keep at it until you feel comfortable—or become convinced that motorcycling is not for you. Once you have acquired the basic riding skills, your next move will be to buy a suitable motorcycle of your own. You are much more likely to learn fast and enjoy it if you pick a small bike for starters—something between 125cc to 350cc. It is important that you can straddle the seat with both feet firmly on the ground. Be sure you can start the bike fairly easily, if it has a kick start, although there is some technique to be acquired here, so don't give up too easily.

I would suggest you buy your first bike from a dealer, to ensure it is in good mechanical order. If you do decide to buy privately, take it to a dealer as soon as possible for a thorough mechanical checkup, preferably before you ride it anywhere. Put as many miles on this machine as you can. Ride it to work, if the traffic is not too difficult; ride it out in the country on weekends and, generally, become familiar with it. Ideally, the machine you choose should be capable of being ridden off the road as well, as riding on poor surfaces is a good way to improve your riding skills. Some more ambitious riders can even learn how to fall—but in no way does dirt riding prepare anyone for coping with the trials and tribulations of road traffic, so this will become the next major part of your training program. It certainly helps here if you have already mastered basic control of your machine, since you will have enough to think about with erratic auto drivers all about you, without having to worry about riding technique as well. Until you have thoroughly mastered the art of defensive riding in an area with which you are familiar, it is rather foolhardy to venture farther afield. It would not be wise to contemplate any serious touring for awhile yet, particularly if your plans include a passenger.

Your next step is to select a touring bike. This is dealt with fully in Chapter 3, while Chapter 4 provides information about the many accessories on the market. In Chapter 5, we look at clothing for the rider and passenger, something else you will need to give careful thought to before you set out on a long trip. Later chapters will help prepare you for the tour itself and answer questions most frequently asked by riders new to touring.

Now let us assume our new rider is no longer a complete novice, but has almost a year's riding and perhaps more than a thousand miles to his credit. This would be a good time to take another riding course—one of the more advanced classes offered locally. If you intend to buy a new motorcycle before you go touring, it would be wise to use it on any riding courses you attend. If no course is available, you should spend time practicing on your own. Try stopping fast, using both front and rear brakes together, until you are absolutely sure you can do it confidently. Fit any new accessories and be sure you know exactly what effect, if any, they have on performance, braking and handling. If possible, load your bike up with all the touring gear and get used to how it feels. If your touring equipment is not yet complete, you can load an equivalent amount of weight onto the appropriate parts of the bike and practice riding like that for the time being. The whole idea is to completely familiarize yourself with the loaded machine in everyday situations, while there is still plenty of time to make adjustments to the bike, accessories or load.

If you are expecting to take a passenger with you, be sure to ride together before you leave. If your passenger has never ridden on a bike before, it is going to take some time before he or she is comfortable on the back of the bike. It is important that you achieve this before you set out on a long tour. It will help if your passenger is dressed properly, since it can be equally cold and wet on the back of the bike as it can be on the front. Added to which, there is often little else to think about as passenger except how uncomfortable you are! This subject is dealt with fairly extensively in Chapters 5 and 6.

Start out by taking your new passenger on short rides, preferably in good weather. Ensure that they are dressed properly and that you have at least the minimum amount of bad-weather gear with you, just in case. Take the time to explain to them exactly what you expect them to do and not to do, where they should grip and what to do in curves and turns. I usually instruct new passengers to sit like a sack of potatoes and do nothing out of the ordinary. Above all, take it easy on the first ride unless they ask you to go faster.

The same rules apply if you have not ridden much with a passenger. Their weight can make a big difference to the bike's handling, especially if they become nervous and lean the wrong way or, even worse, if they ride themselves and try to "assist" your riding technique. Take it very easy until you are completely confident that you can predict exactly what your passenger and your bike will do under different circumstances.

Not only do the activities associated with touring require good physical condition for maximum enjoyment, but all-day rides are equally demanding. Being in shape means being able to enjoy the whole day, and the full range of activities that go along with motorcycle touring.

Now you are ready to put the two major loads together on the machine—your passenger and all equipment. Hopefully, you will have done all your weight calculations and practice rides, so you will know what to expect from your fully loaded motorcycle. Even so, it can sometimes come as a surprise, especially the first time out. If you have the time and inclination, it can be well worth loading up the bike with all your touring gear and heading off for a day or two, staying out overnight. This gives you a chance to try out your loaded machine on unknown roads, as well as providing an opportunity for you to test any new camping gear. Ideally, you will experience some rain and cold weather, which will enable you to check out your rainsuits; it is no joke finding out that they leak when you are hundreds of miles away from home.

So far we have concentrated on the preparation of your machine, riding skills and such, but there is at least one other area of preparation that you should consider. Take a look at yourself. What kind of physical shape are you in? You do not need to be fit enough for the New York City Marathon in order to go motorcycle touring, but it does not hurt to be in reasonable condition. It can be quite tiring to ride all day and then have to set up camp at night. By the time you have built a campfire and squatted beside it to do the cooking, you are likely to be aware of several muscles you did not know you had. Even riding alone can be quite demanding at times, particularly in bad weather. Heavy crosswinds are especially exhausting, since they can strain many different parts of the body at once, and this will tire you out very rapidly if you are not physically strong and fairly fit.

Almost any form of regular exercise will help increase your fitness level, which in turn is almost certain to increase your overall enjoyment of touring and camping. Even those last few hours of a long riding day can become quite tolerable.

I enjoy jogging and find it easy to continue with it while I am away touring, since it requires little specialized equipment. Basically, all you need is a pair of running shoes, since your swimsuit and T-shirts will serve as your running outfit for most of the time. One unexpected bonus can be a weight loss, which will be a big help if you have an overloading problem on your motorcycle. If you are traveling two-up and both start exercising, you could conceivably find yourselves with an additional 20 pounds or so of load capacity!

It may sound like rather a lot of effort and hard work to prepare yourself for touring, but I've not yet met anyone who has regretted it. So, put your machine *and* yourself into top shape—and go!

Chapter 3
Selecting a Motorcycle for Touring

The motorcycle you choose for touring is important, but not *all* important. Exceptionally enjoyable tours are possible on machines not really suited to touring—that is, motorcycles that are too small or that may have too much vibration.

This was best demonstrated to me recently when I met a man in his sixties in Ft. Stockton, Texas. He was on his way to California from Florida . . . riding a Honda 180cc motorcycle loaded with what he needed to make the trip. Not only was he making do with this small motorcycle, he was having the time of his life! This part of the country is characterized by immense open spaces and great distances between towns. But he was keeping his pace moderate and daily travel distances low—200 miles or so.

Touring on an ill-suited machine brings out an important fact that applies to any motorcycle chosen for touring: the rider must determine the machine's limitations and stay within them. This is true regardless of whether the machine was recently purchased, new or used, or if it has been "in the family" for some time and employed for commuting, sport riding or other short-distance uses.

If the motorcycle chosen for touring lacks long-distance comfort, keep distances between stops short. If it lacks weight capacity, keep loads light. Installation of accessories or parts such as custom seats and replacement rear suspensions can be made on almost any motorcycle, for considerable improvement in comfort and handling. However, one item clearly not acceptable is *poor condition* of engine, drivetrain, brakes, tires or lights. If the motorcycle is mechanically sound and you know its limitations (and are willing to live with them), nearly any street-legal machine can be used for touring.

One of the unique features of touring in the United States is the combination of straight roads and vast distances in so much of the country. Europeans are amazed at our motorcycles—especially the amount of equipment seen on so many touring machines. What they fail to take into consideration is the vast difference in conditions and heritage. But at least the Europeans go touring for considerable distances, so they can appreciate how our bikes have evolved, especially after they have spent a day or two on the interstate crossing one of the prairie states. But our touring conditions are almost beyond the comprehension of the Japanese, and that includes the manufacturers of all the major motorcycles; there simply is nothing in their sphere of experience to explain touring in this country.

Not only do we have a very real wanderlust/exploration heritage in this country, it has been popularized in our media to the point where it has become an accepted part of our lives. No other country has the road system that America can boast, nor the distances and variety of topography all accessible via these first-class roads. For the touring rider who wants to see as much of the U.S. as possible from the saddle of a motorcycle, the distances simply have to be taken into consideration. If it's done right, vast distances and great open spaces can be fully appreciated—even savored—as the magnificent heritage they represent for Americans.

Distance is why riding comfort plays such an important role in selection of a machine. Riding across 800 miles of straight road with very slowly changing topography can easily turn into an endurance test if the rider is uncomfortable and just trying to "get it over with." But it can be enjoyed and appreciated by the rider who is relaxed and comfortable. Who says adventure has to be uncomfortable? Each person must decide the type of touring which is most appealing.

Before even shopping for a motorcycle, define your needs. Model selection, like most things having to do with motorcycles, is an emotion-charged issue. The final choice will probably be influenced, if not dictated, by emotion (that certainly includes styling) but at least if we start from a solid base of functional requirements we can narrow the field down to machines that stand a good chance of filling our needs, both practical and aesthetic.

A major consideration is money. It will have a bearing on whether we buy a new machine, a "new" used one or keep the old one. Don't forget to consider the cost of other equipment needed for touring—bike accessories, riding clothes, camping equipment and first-year travel costs. The bike will be a big-ticket item, but these other items can combine to present a sizable total and they should be included. We'll consider cost later. The first priority is getting a fix on your individual requirements for a motorcycle, then deciding how you can satisfy these requirements within the budget. There really is no overriding cost factor. Some requirements are more critical than others and offer more latitude, but each point is important and should be considered in conjunction with all the other factors involved.

A major consideration is whether you will be touring solo or two-up. If two-up, the weight and space represented by the second person must be considered, and luggage requirements will probably double. While having a passenger is the single largest weight consideration, camping gear will add weight. In fact, two-up riders who will be camping represent the highest weight figures touring bikes are required to carry. These travelers not only face the most stringent weight limitations on gear and accessories, they also require larger motorcycles.

The most obvious relationship of load to motorcycle size requirement is one of engine power, but this point is secondary to the machine's capacity to comfortably carry the required weight. This is governed by wheelbase and the gross vehicle weight

Staying within a bike's limitations means selecting lighter accessories and smaller touring loads for the smaller machines. But it also means staying within the GVWR (gross vehicle weight rating) of even the largest of motorcycles to ensure safety and riding comfort.

rating (GVWR), which is how much weight the manufacturer states the bike can accommodate. Wheelbase is important because it will govern where the passenger's weight and most of the luggage will be positioned in relationship to the rear axle. (See Chapter 9, *Loading*, for more details on GVWR and load-to-wheelbase relationships.) These two items are directly related to engine size—i.e., the large-engine bikes tend to have the longest wheelbases and the largest load ratings.

Why are weight capacity and wheelbase important? Because they have a direct bearing on how manageable and pleasant the bike is to ride when loaded. Engine size and power will hinge more on personal preference than any actual requirement. Anything from about 400cc or larger, with a five- or six-speed transmission, will provide enough power to get two people and all their gear over any paved road in the United States—the only disadvantages of smaller machines being a loss of time, more shifting of gears and less speed. Unfortunately, medium to small bikes (under 700cc) generally offer neither the wheelbase nor GVWR needed for serious two-up touring, especially with camping gear.

After reading the chapters on accessories, clothing and camping, you can pretty well define your weight requirements. The figure will consist of the rider and passenger weight (if applicable) added to the weight of the bike and its accessories, plus the weight of everything to be carried. For those riders new to touring, much of this will have to be estimated. But each of the chapters listed above includes weight information that will help make your estimates reasonably accurate.

TABLE 1: To get a feel for weight and size, the following table indicates weight capacity and wheelbase vs. engine size. This doesn't apply to any particular machine, but is a generalized table incorporating all the bikes in the various size categories, whereas actual models may differ.

Size	Weight Capacity	Wheelbase
	(GVWR minus bike weight)	
400-450cc	375 lbs.	55″
500-550cc	380 lbs.	56″
600-650cc	400 lbs.	57″
700-750cc	440 lbs.	59″
800-850cc	445 lbs.	59″
900-950cc	450 lbs.	61″
1000-1200cc	470 lbs.	62″
1200cc & over	490 lbs.	63″

While there are additional considerations besides weight and cost, these two will dominate the conversation during motorcycle shopping trips—so let's examine them more closely. Since cost, weight capacity and bike size are interrelated, your decisions regarding each will influence the final choice of bike required for your brand of touring. As outlined above, the amount of weight to be carried will be extremely important in selecting the best size, but other considerations should influence your thinking. Your experience level is an important factor. For instance, perhaps all requirements suggest the largest bike available but your experience is very limited and the weight, power and sheer size of the superbikes make you uncomfortable. Related to this is your physical size—mainly, how long your legs are. But this is becoming less of a problem as manufacturers continue to lower seat height through bike design and styling trends. Several of the largest late models are available with seat height comparable to 400cc machines.

If seat height is important for you, be sure to check the models designated Special or Custom—the ones that have something of a "chopper" appearance. Some sacrifices are unavoidable with this style—mainly smaller fuel tank size. But this will be covered in detail a little later in this chapter.

While physical size will play a role in your ability to handle a particular bike size, confidence and experience are more important factors. Out on the road, a person of virtually any size can ride the largest motorcycles as long as they can reach the controls. Problems with bike size and weight begin when one stops. Just holding the bike up for a stoplight presents very serious problems if both feet don't touch the ground. As weight increases, pushing the machine into or out of parking positions grows more difficult. Touring equipment, accessories and luggage will appreciably increase total weight. Most of the big machines will top 1,000 pounds when loaded with two people, a full complement of accessories and touring gear. Of course, pushing maneuvers are performed without the weight of riders. Even so, you could easily find yourself with some 700 or 800 pounds of motorcycle to push around. This being the case, a smaller bike makes sense for anyone of small stature or limited experience.

In Chapter 2 we covered the different approaches to gaining riding experience. It might be worth your while to incorporate some of those ideas in your plans, if bike size is going to be unduly affected by your physical limitations and/or lack of riding experience.

Regardless of experience or physical size, the type of touring you find most attractive should definitely have a bearing on the size of bike selected. If your thinking runs more to relatively short, regional tours—say, less than a week at a time with daily riding distances of 100 to 200 miles—the topography of your home area will also affect your choice. For instance, residents of the Northeast can choose any number of outstanding areas that are easily accessible. They offer a great deal of riding on two-lane roads with plenty of curves.

On the other hand, a rider living in one of the prairie states could regularly knock off 1,000 miles the first couple of days just getting to the tour area. Usually, this kind of travel is done on interstate highways where large motorcycle size is a definite advantage. Conversely, poking along a narrow, curving mountain road with lots of stops is more pleasant on a smaller, lighter machine. If your interests also include riding dirt or gravel roads with any degree of regularity, a smaller bike should be considered.

To put this into better perspective, let's look at fairly specific but hypothetical examples:

Couple A lives in the Midwest. They want to tour two-up, and he has quite a bit of riding experience, including time spent on a fully equipped 1000cc machine. They want to include camping, some hiking and plenty of sightseeing in their touring. They want a full frame-mounted fairing and saddlebags. He weighs 185 pounds; she weighs 115. An additional 15 pounds per person for clothing, helmets and boots yields a combined weight of 330 pounds. They figure 28 pounds for camping gear (they already own it and know the exact weight), 25 pounds for riding suits, rainwear, extra gloves and additional riding gear. Other clothes will add about 30 pounds for the two of them, and they figure in 25 pounds for assorted items like cameras and sports equipment, making a total of 108 pounds. Adding 70 pounds for bike accessories, they come up with a grand total of 508 pounds. Now if we refer back to Table 1, we can see they will fall into the 1200cc and oversize group (actually slightly heavy even for that class). But as can be seen from the table, the difference between each successive engine size as it relates to weight capacity and wheelbase is quite small—significant, but small. By trimming 50 pounds off their total load, they can comfortably select nearly any bike down to and including a 750cc model. But they plan to be spending a fair portion of their time on interstate-type roads (remember, they live in the Midwest), and they like the comfort and power of the larger bikes. Also, the cost doesn't bother them and he finds the larger machines pleasant to handle.

We can see that any number of factors open to change could influence the selection. For instance, if we put a dollar limitation on the bike selection, they can lower the size to around 900cc without a major sacrifice (just two inches lost in wheelbase and some 40 pounds or so in weight capacity). The bike will still be large, very powerful and able to cover great distances in comfort and style.

Another example follows the other extreme. Let's say John is a college student in the Northeast and has very limited income. He has all summer free for touring and wants to go it alone. He has owned several bikes, all under 650cc, but needs a new one. He plans to camp every night and wants to do quite a bit of backpacking and fishing. He weighs 150 pounds (165 dressed for riding) and has much equipment to take along— say another 150 pounds of gear. He wants protection from the wind, but doesn't really care what other accessories he has, as long as they get the job done. He opts for a set of throw-over saddlebags, a big tank bag and his backpack lashed on the seat behind him for luggage, plus a clear plexiglass fairing for wind protection. We can figure 10 pounds for the fairing, and about 20 pounds for the different bags, so John's total is 345 pounds. Since cost is a major factor, and time isn't, one of the fine little 400-450cc machines would be ideal for him. The 400-class bikes are all vertical twins, so vibration will be a slight problem. This size bike isn't especially big on comfort, but the time aspect in this example allows frequent stops and no fixed schedule, so the comfort

The smaller, lighter and more maneuverable machines are especially suited to riding on curving roads, while the larger touring models may provide better riding and greater comfort on long, flat stretches of highway. Where you plan to do most of your touring could be a deciding factor in your selection of a bike.

obstacle is fairly easily overcome.

If we change the scenario slightly—increase the budget a bit, but cut back on time—it would suggest moving up the size scale to the 500cc class or even up to a 650, adding a small frame-mounted fairing but leaving everything else the same. In the 650s, we not only have four-cylinder bikes from which to choose, but several offer very desirable touring features like shaft drive. Comfort takes a significant jump and operating expenses are only mildly affected. In fact, the bikes that fall between 500 and 650cc are some of the nicest solo touring mounts available. They are light and easily handled; they make reasonably good gravel road bikes, yet will cover long distances on the interstate with ease and comfort for the rider. In the mountains they will require more shifting than the larger-engine bikes and won't provide the acceleration for passing, especially at higher elevations and when loaded for touring. The best of the large bikes will ride noticeably smoother than the best machines below 650cc.

The implication so far is that riders going solo can select nearly any size bike (true), but that two-up touring riders will need a "big" bike (false). A 400cc bike can be used for two-up touring. But here is where we get back to operating within the machine's limitations, and the 400-class machines will present stringent restrictions for two-up touring riders.

These restrictions begin with size and weight of riders; if they are big people there will be virtually no capacity left for anything else. Also, the short wheelbase will exaggerate the weight of anything carried, including the passenger. This doesn't mean that two-up touring on a 400-class bike can't be done, or even that it shouldn't be done. But riders who select this size motorcycle, for whatever reason, should be aware that it presents problems. Rather than detail the problems presented by this combination, let's examine the desirable attributes of any bike for touring and compare each size class to see how they measure up. These attributes will also assist in selecting a particular model from within the most desirable size group. The desirable features aren't in any particular order because each rider must decide individually which features best apply to his needs.

Reliability and Maintenance

Modern motorcycles are becoming as reliable as modern automobiles, and many are as complex. Who will do maintenance on the bike, the dealer or the owner? The more cylinders a bike has, in general, the more complex the maintenance. Regardless of who does the maintenance, it will be expensive. If it's by the owner, most of the cost is in time. If by a dealer, it's measured in money. In either respect, maintenance must be considered (especially from the cost angle). Reliability of a motorcycle is usually more dependent on proper maintenance than any other single factor. Any one of the current crop of motorcycles, reasonably well maintained, offers a high degree of reliability.

A number of features reduce maintenance and improve reliability. Probably the most popular for touring is shaft drive. It eliminates the single item requiring the most maintenance—the chain. In addition to eliminating all the lubricating and adjusting chores of chain drive, shaft drive is generally cleaner and quieter, but is reputed to take slightly more power to drive than a chain. A more significant drawback, other than generally higher cost, is that bikes with shaft drive usually weigh 30 to 50 pounds more, except those models which are the lightest of the big bikes.

Another item that affects reliability and maintenance (or lack of it) is cast alloy wheels. Wire spoke wheels require occasional maintenance to keep them true and they can cause problems under heavy-load touring conditions. Nearly all manufacturers have gone to cast alloy wheels on touring models, and I'm glad to see this change because it has ushered in tubeless tires, which reduce the probability of blowouts. They also correct the weight problem and eliminate the cost of inner tubes. What's more, cast alloy wheels are much easier to keep clean.

Styling

In years past, styling meant the shape of the fuel tank and side panels, along with small details. Now, distinctly different styles of motorcycles are sold. In the past, the Japanese bikes had a certain "look," which Honda calls "traditional." In 1978, Yamaha introduced their XS650 and XS750 bikes as *Specials* and they were an instant sales success. Since that time all the Japanese manufacturers have introduced their versions of the Special or custom-style bike. These bikes exhibit several features that characterize the styling theme. A major feature is seating position, as indicated by handlebars and seat. Seating position is nearly upright on some models, or even leaned back slightly. This is achieved by buckhorn-style, pullback handlebars and a seat mounted as low as the frame design will permit. Lowered seat height is a real advantage for some, and is nice with a loaded bike, as it makes it easier to manage when stopped. But lowering the seat changes the seat-to-peg relationship and puts the feet higher relative to the seat, producing a sharper bend at the knees—less comfortable for long distances. The upright position is quite comfortable at low speeds or behind a fairing or windshield; but without wind protection, it becomes a rather unpleasant job to hold yourself upright against the force of the wind. When the style gets a little too exaggerated and creates a slightly leaned-back position, it proves to be uncomfortable for long distance regardless of wind protection.

There are other styling characteristics, such as the fat rear tire and abbreviated, megaphone-style upswept exhaust pipes. Both look good to most riders, but the fat rear tire does more harm than good for handling and is usually slightly smaller in diameter than stock, effectively lowering the overall gear ratio. The engine turns faster for a given road speed. The exhaust pipes tend to interfere with the mounting of saddlebags. In fact, some bags just won't fit this style bike.

The single most obvious styling feature—the one that causes the most problems for touring—is the fuel tank. It tends to be small, so driving range is reduced.

Other minor styling features usually have only slight effect on a motorcycle's performance for touring. Several models have simpler instrumentation than the same model with conventional styling. Unless the lowered seat height is of major importance, the Custom or Special is generally somewhat less suited to long-distance touring than the conventional-style machine. In most cases there are a couple of models in each style—the same frame, engine and drivetrain, but with major cosmetic differences. One model will be the Custom or Special while the other will be the more conventional style. This is not true in all cases; recently some new models have been introduced in Custom or Special trim only. Actually, the new Custom or Special bikes are influencing most manufacturers' entire product line, so bikes designated as "touring models" are showing up with lowered seat height and larger rear tires, among other things. While styling is pretty much a matter of personal preference, when it affects the functional areas of bike design like seating position, fuel tank size and tire size, the question goes beyond pure styling and the bike should be evaluated on function.

Comfort

Rider and passenger comfort is an enormously subjective matter, especially in regard to seat and riding position. This is one reason a great many accessories on the market are aimed at changing seating position or the seat itself. It's virtually impossible to tell if a seat will be comfortable by looking at it, or by sitting on it in a dealer's showroom. Magazine tour tests are probably the best source of information on seat comfort for any particular model, but even here it's subjective by necessity. Seats are getting better on models specifically designed for touring, but beware of seats that are narrow or have fairly sharp, well-defined edges because these edges can really dig into the inner thigh after a few hours. A number of remedies for an uncomfortable seat are listed in the chapter on touring accessories. As for riding position, this can be checked in a dealer's showroom by sitting on the bike.

If you plan to use a fairing or windshield, sitting on the bike will help determine if it will be comfortable. But if you don't, quite a bit of forward lean will be required for comfort on the road and this will not feel right when sitting still. Check actual passenger space on the seat if you will be riding two-up most of the time.

An item that will be important to long-distance comfort is vibration. As a general rule, the more cylinders, the less vibration. But engine configuration plays a big part, as well. Singles tend to produce the most vibration, followed by vertical twins, then "V" or opposed twins. Triples generally feel more like V-twins. Currently, the smoothest models are either flat opposed fours or in-line sixes. There are a couple of items that can alter this general assessment. The first is use of balancers—extra weights designed into the engine to partially offset rotational imbalances. They're used mostly in singles and vertical twins. The other is rubber mounting of the engine. This is becoming quite popular again and can be extremely effective and can sometimes virtually eliminate vibration felt by the rider. The engine still produces vibration, but it simply isn't felt by the rider or passenger. (A minor exception is the passenger's feet, which still get a little tingle on some models.)

Probably the most important consideration regarding a bike that vibrates is the rpm range where highest intensity occurs. Usually, the range is quite narrow. If the worst vibration occurs in your normal cruising range, this can detract from an otherwise fine touring mount.

Special

The highly styled Special (Custom) bike is shown at left. At right, the Japanese or European style bike, and below, the "Traditional" touring motorcycle.

Japanese Style

Touring Bike

A major comfort consideration is how well the bike handles irregularities in the road surface—bumps, potholes and rail crossings. A smooth ride will add greatly to long-distance comfort. Front as well as rear suspension are important for a good ride, and some big improvements have been made in this area in the last few years. A problem for the touring rider is that most motorcycle suspensions are quite load-sensitive. The suspension may be fine with a light load but poor with a full load of accessories, people and touring gear. That's why we are seeing more models with air-assisted suspensions front and rear. While air isn't perfect, it certainly offers the adjustability needed for those who use their bikes alternately in light and heavy load configurations. Air-adjustable suspension is especially critical at the rear, but it works well at the front to compensate for the weight of a frame-mounted fairing or any other added weight.

Performance and Operation

The first thing that comes to mind under the performance heading is probably acceleration. While it's one of the more exciting aspects of motorcycling, it's certainly not the entire performance picture. Obviously, acceleration is directly tied to engine size, but it's also related to weight. As engine size increases, so does weight, although differences aren't as great as one might expect.

Acceleration of the larger engine is really welcome in a touring bike while passing other vehicles on a two-lane road. Here again, the two-up touring rider will get the most benefit from the increased power of the larger engine. When the weight of accessories, a passenger and touring gear is added—in other words, when a bike is loaded to its maximum weight rating—the weight will have less effect on a big bike's performance than on a smaller bike, with the dividing line at about the 750ccs, depending on the particular model.

In actual practice, straight-line acceleration from a standing start isn't especially important, but it normally goes hand in hand with the kind of acceleration that *is* important—passing power. Most of the really enjoyable touring is done on meandering two-lane roads where passing is common, so the ability to do it quickly and safely with a loaded bike is most important.

Another aspect of the big vs. small engine is the rpm at normal cruising speeds. The larger engine can be geared higher to turn less engine rpm at 55 to 60 mph. Touring is more relaxed, generally quieter and there is less vibration.

The other side of the performance coin is handling and stopping. Here the greater size and weight of the bigger bike is a detriment; differences are small, but discernible. Accessories and touring loads narrow the gap, especially in handling, so it boils down to a question of proper suspension rather than a question of size. The major exception is handling at very slow speed (under 10 mph) when sheer weight takes over and the bigger and heavier bike will be more of a handful. Here, as in all aspects of motorcycle riding, experience and knowledge will pay big dividends in ease of operation. For instance, I have seen inexperienced touring riders head a loaded bike into the curb on a downhill slant, which is not smart because they must push it back uphill. But if the rider had backed into that kind of parking spot, it would have been just a matter of starting the engine and riding away.

Experience and knowledge are the answer when managing a bike loaded for touring. This also applies to traveling curves at highway speeds. A bike with proper suspension for touring loads not only retains a good ride but will keep a good portion of its cornering clearance and manageability in curves, making it nearly as pleasant to ride on curving roads as a bare bike. Certainly, speeds will be reduced according to load, but this is where a highly adjustable air suspension pays real dividends by allowing normal ride height with a loaded bike.

While acceleration and handling are important facets of a bike's performance, another critically important aspect is its stopping power. As weight increases with passenger and/or touring gear, brakes are pressed into more severe service. Stopping distances are increased by adding weight, making dual-disc front brakes and single-disc rear brakes especially attractive. The only penalty paid for disc brakes is some initial loss of braking power in wet weather, but this is improving with each year's crop of new bikes. Brake pad material appears to be the most important factor in wet weather braking.

Even more important than the type of brakes is their operation; they should be as smooth and progressive as possible, so additional hand or foot pressure results in a parallel increase in brake action. The amount of effort required for a given amount of brake action is not as important as its being progressive. A soft or stiff brake can be handled through experience, but erratic action diminishes the predictability needed for minimum stopping distances.

In addition to smooth brakes, a light clutch and smooth transmission are most desirable, along with a lack of drive-line slack. These items, combined, will aid greatly in smooth operation—especially important for the peace of mind and comfort of a passenger.

Other items to take into consideration are lights (halogen type are best), horn (as load as possible) and stands. Side and center stands take on a whole new importance when a bike is loaded with accessories and touring gear. Here again, suspension plays a part; a rear suspension that squats down excessively under a load will change the angle of the side stand, leaving the bike too upright in most cases and making the center stand difficult to use.

One aspect of performance is coming under ever-increasing interest: fuel consumption. Poor gas mileage not only costs money, but it reduces fuel range—which is an important consideration for touring. Lack of fuel range will limit the touring rider's freedom, especially in days of short supplies and reduced operating hours in many service stations. Lack of fuel range will mean not being able to ride late at night or very early in the morning in some areas.

Overall range depends on consumption and tank size. But what constitutes good mileage and range? Actually, fuel consumption is as much governed by the rider (speed and riding style) as by the bike. Most will agree that high speeds and fast acceleration will drastically reduce fuel economy on some bikes, but big fairings will also cost mpg at highway speeds. On bikes 1000cc and over, it's no big trick to get mileage in the low

30s with heavy loads, high speeds and hard riding. We do it all the time on tour tests, which are by necessity hard miles. But the same bike with the same load, ridden more conservatively, will repay the rider with fuel consumption figures in the high 40s—quite a difference.

The rider who selects the Special or Custom-style bike really pays a penalty in fuel tank size. Let's assume a particular bike, rider and load combination gets 42 mpg on a fairly regular basis (realizing that high altitude and plenty of hills, heavy headwinds or higher than normal speeds will reduce this figure). But by using 42 mpg as an average, we can calculate the difference between a four-gallon tank and a five-gallon model. Obviously, it will be 42 miles. But that's not the total picture. Let's assume both bikes go on reserve with 6/10-gallon remaining in the tank, or about 25 miles. I'm not especially fond of running a bike until it goes on reserve, so I generally add about 25 miles to that figure, allowing for greater consumption between fill-ups, or perhaps a closed station where I had planned to fill up.

While total range is 168 miles for the four-gallon tank and 210 miles for the five, reducing this by the 50-mile cushion results in 118 and 160 miles, respectively. Certain circumstances can further reduce this figure—for instance, traveling back roads where stations aren't as frequent, traveling on a Sunday or crossing the desert. If I see a station open and I've ridden a bike with a four-gallon tank about 100 miles, I'll fill up—as I would with the five-gallon model if it's around the 150-mile mark. On a long 600-mile day, that's two extra gas stops for the smaller tank, and if we figure about 30 minutes per stop, an hour is spent hanging around filling stations—not my idea of fun.

A fuel gauge can help by indicating (other than miles traveled) how much fuel is actually left in the tank. If we increase the tank size to six or even seven gallons, we get into some real driving range. Still using the 42 mpg figure, a 6.5-gallon tank gives us a maximum range of 273 miles, or a working range of 200-plus miles. Then, if we can increase fuel economy to 50 mpg—not out of the question by any means—we get a working range with the 6.5-gallon tank that's well over 250 miles. With that kind of range, gas stops become a negligible factor except under extreme conditions. Fuel range is a major consideration in selecting a touring bike and should be examined carefully if touring is your main purpose.

Dealers and Accessories

Assume you have figured what you want in a bike, including weight capacity, engine size and all the lesser features such as shaft drive and air suspension. You even know what kind of accessories you prefer. You have studied all the magazine tests and have narrowed the choice down to two or three models of different brands. Now might be a good time to take a critical look at dealers—not just the one from whom you will be purchasing the bike, but the total number of dealers for this particular brand.

The touring rider is especially dependent on the size of a dealer network for parts and service while on the road. Harley-Davidson, Honda, Yamaha, Kawasaki, Suzuki and BMW all have solid dealer networks in this country, while the rider who selects a Moto Guzzi might have to do a little searching for a dealer. Those who select other brands should expect difficulty in finding a dealer in anything less than a major metropolitan area.

The other dealer-oriented question is: which one will be best for you locally? This will be the dealer with whom you will have the most contact.

What is a good dealer? That's a tough question—but you should get at least a partial answer before you purchase your motorcycle. If you already have a bike, try taking it in for minor service and note how you are treated. Asking other riders is a traditional method, too. It isn't always successful, but it's certainly worth a try, especially if you select current service customers.

Check the relative size and condition of the three major working areas in the dealership—sales, parts and service—as this will give you some idea of where the dealer places the most emphasis. Beware of those with big, shiny sales rooms and skimpy parts and service departments. The inventory of new motorcycles and types of accessories will also give you an idea of the type of dealer you'll be doing business with. Usually, the best bet is a dealership that is oriented toward touring.

If the motorcycle you select isn't factory-equipped with all the accessories you want, it's a good idea to select a dealer who handles that equipment as well as the bike you choose. This has a couple of advantages. If you are purchasing the bike and all the accessories at one time, the dealer can often offer a substantial price break on the total package. Also, it's a time-saver if one dealer is responsible for *all* warranty work.

If you have decided on a particular accessory, make sure it's available for the various motorcycle models you will be considering. In some cases, many accessories aren't available for new bikes early in the model year, so if it's important, put it on the checklist. This also applies to combinations of accessories. For example, certain accessories won't work with other items like saddlebags and luggage racks. Engine guard bars won't work with some fairings.

In summary, selecting just the right touring bike for your needs is not difficult. Figure out how much weight capacity you will need most of the time (total weight of accessories, rider-passenger weight and gear to be used on most trips). Then check this figure against the weight capacities of the various models. Don't forget to consider where and how the weight will be carried—and be sure to ask yourself if the wheelbase and power are adequate for your kind of riding. Remember to check on fuel capacity and fuel range; the more the better for most touring needs.

Then, with the right dealer, put together your dream machine and you have basic ingredients for some of the most exciting travel adventures to be had anywhere in the world . . . motorcycle touring right here in the USA.

Chapter 4
Touring Accessories

For many riders, a touring bike is any motorcycle equipped with a fairing and saddlebags. While defining a touring cycle is not that simple, it is true that specific accessories will make a motorcycle better suited to a particular type of riding—in this case, touring. Manufacturers are discovering what most riders have known for years, and they are now offering "touring models" sold with a full set of standard or optional accessories designed exclusively for touring purposes.

In some cases, selecting the model that's fully equipped will save a little time and effort (not having to select the accessories you want) and, in many cases, will cost a few dollars less than putting the same package together separately. But a pre-package touring bike does present some disadvantages—the most obvious being that your bike will look like several thousand others. The real disadvantage is that in most cases the manufacturer's selection is not necessarily the best possible combination for your particular needs. Selecting appropriate touring accessories is the topic of this chapter, which is written to assist you in relating your needs to the different types of accessories available.

Wind Protection

One of the first things a new rider discovers about motorcycling is how great the wind feels; that is, until the first long ride or the weather turns cold. Then, all of a sudden, it's possible to get too much of a good thing. Various forms of wind protection devices are designed to be installed on motorcycles. But before we discuss the various types and their advantages and disadvantages, let's examine the case for any form of wind protection.

The list of benefits offered by a windshield or fairing is impressive, but certain compromises must be considered. Two major benefits are offered by any form of wind protection device. The first is reduction of fatigue by reducing or eliminating the force of the wind on the chest, with its resulting strain on the muscles of the arms, shoulders and back. Another benefit is protection from the weather. A windshield or fairing cuts the chilling effect of the wind, and will also help deflect rain.

In some respects, a windshield or fairing is the warmest article of "clothing" one can select. Obviously, it's not an actual article of clothing, but it certainly will have a bearing on how much you will have to wear in cold weather. This effect is greater as temperature drops. Below 10 degrees F., it's almost impossible to keep warm on a bike at highway speeds without some form of wind protection. One of the joys of touring is the feeling of oneness with the surrounding environment. You've missed half the trip if you haven't looked around you at the passing farms and valleys, each with a story to tell in rich colors and smells. But your perspective of what's going on around you can be severely hampered if you're unable to turn your head without worrying about the force of the wind, which can be enough to knock off your glasses if you don't have a face shield. You may feel compelled to keep your eyes on the road to spot flying debris or to dodge insects. One or two head-wrenching blasts may be all it takes to convince you that long distance touring is best done with some form of wind protection.

There is a great deal of similar logic behind using wind protection and wearing comfortable clothing. If the rider is relaxed and physically comfortable, I believe he or she is more inclined to be alert—either to spectacular scenery or to a developing traffic situation. Staying alert is the key to safe riding and the key to staying alert is to achieve the optimum in riding comfort for sustained periods of time. This is why dressing properly is so important (for more on this subject, read Chapter 5). Windshields come in handy for other things as well, as any bug-splattered biker will tell you. (An alternative to windshields is wearing a face shield with your three-quarter or full-coverage helmet, but I have always found the face shield to be very confining, and I actually enjoy a bit of wind in my face.) A windshield ensures that I won't be hit by flying bugs and debris, and as long as the windshield is low enough to see over, my visibility is not severely limited. With a windshield or fairing, a rider can remove the face shield and still ride in relative comfort, even when looking over the top of the windshield.

I find it preferable to mount any windscreen so the top edge just about lines up with my chin when I'm sitting in a relaxed position on the bike. That way I look over it at all times, unless I deliberately lean down behind it when riding through heavy rain or a swarm of insects. With a lowered windshield you will occasionally get hit in the face with rain and bugs, but I feel it's a worthwhile concession for the improved vision I get. It's also a matter of personal preference; I simply don't like looking through anything, except my glasses, when riding. But there is a very practical reason: improved vision, especially if the windshield is dirty or scratched. It only takes one early morning start with a heavily frosted windshield that won't stay clear, no matter how many times it's wiped clean, for one to fully appreciate good vision.

The most common windshield material is plexiglass. It is a relatively simple task to cut it to the desired height. With windshield or fairing mounted on the bike, mark on the windshield where you want the top to be when you are sitting on the bike. Then, remove the windshield and use masking tape on both sides to mark the line where you want to cut it. A power sabre or hacksaw can be used to make the cut, and a knife can be used as a scraper to round the edge to its original radius. In the long run, it is simpler to order the proper height windscreen from the manufacturer; most offer optional sizes and some fairings have adjustable windshields. Choosing to look over or through a windshield is a personal decision; looking through offers better protection, while looking over affords better vision.

Wind protection offers a number of benefits, depending on the particular type of wind protector you choose. There are also some obvious characteristics of each type that are less than advantageous. For if a fairing or windshield is most welcome when the weather turns cold, they can make riding downright sweaty when the weather is hot. But that's not a major drawback. The most important consideration is the adverse effect most windshields and fairings have on handling. This, of course, will depend considerably on the type and model of wind protector, the size and model of bike it's mounted on, as well as weather conditions and road speed. One other factor that might be considered a disadvantage, at least by some, is the cost of wind protection. Like everything else, it keeps going up.

Frame-mounted Fairings

This type of fairing is an American-style accessory. It was developed here, and the United States is still the major market for this kind of fairing. The typical version of the large frame-mounted fairing is, strictly speaking, a three-quarter style fairing, but nearly all manufacturers now offer add-on lower units as standard or optional equipment, and they effectively turn it into a full fairing, making the point rather academic.

Craig Vetter started development on this "American"-style fairing in his living room around 1967. His Windjammer fairing has changed the appearance of American motorcyling. He used fiberglass and then ABS plastic, which offered a number of advantages over fiberglass. It's relatively lightweight, withstands most falls without breaking and is easy to form into the needed shapes. It also holds up well to vibration and the weather. Today, nearly every fairing is made of ABS plastic.

Another characteristic of this type of fairing developed by Vetter is the storage space inside. This is achieved by making the fairing from two separate pieces, one for the exterior and one for the interior part that faces the rider. While Craig Vetter developed this style fairing, you have to hand it to American riders who knew a good thing when they saw it. This style fairing offers outstanding rider protection,—in most instances, the best available. Usually it is quite large, in comparison with other forms of wind protection. Most of the frame-mounted, three-quarter fairings are 32 to 35 inches wide at their widest point directly in front of the handlebars. This affords good protection for hands. These fairings weigh 25 to 35 pounds, but some models go as high as 50 pounds when optional accessories are included. Those figures include the hardware used to mount the fairing.

In addition to providing excellent rider protection, large frame-mounted fairings provide additional visual bulk, making riders more visible to other motorists. Studies indicate that light-colored fairings, especially white, stand out from the background better than the darker colors. Protection and visual impact are relative to size. To a large extent, this applies to fuel consumption as well, because fairings simply present more frontal area for the motorcycle to push. While actual fuel consumption will depend on many factors, such as engine size, speed and riding style, a large fairing can be expected to reduce overall mileage figures by at least a couple of miles per gallon.

This style fairing also offers some well-placed, weather-protected storage. The only precaution is to avoid placing heavy items in the fairing. I try to keep the fairing load down to around 10 pounds. Since all the weight of a fairing and its load are placed on the front of the bike, use of a fairing frequently calls for minor suspension alterations. This is where the relatively new air forks work so well; it's a simple matter to raise air pressure a few pounds to compensate for the extra weight. On older bikes, optional front springs are available to raise the ride height to compensate for the added weight.

The frame-mounted fairing offers a convenient mounting point for any number of additional accessories, including radios, auxiliary instruments and radar detectors, all of which will add more weight to the front of the bike. Many fairings can be ordered to color-match the most popular bikes, which makes for a really striking effect. Fairings offered by the individual motorcycle manufacturers are usually designed and color-matched to complement a particular model, which is an accessory option to consider.

Fairings affect bike handling in two ways. The first is from the wind, mainly cross-winds, because the fairing offers a larger surface area for the wind to strike. The other is weight, as any added weight tends to adversely affect bike handling, which means you will feel that extra 25 to 50 pounds when you go around fast corners. Generally, however, the effect of weight is nominal and won't be a factor for most riders at normal touring speeds; and crosswinds will have little bearing on steering with the frame-mounted fairings because the front fork is not affected by the wind as it is with fork or handlebar-mounted fairings. Keep in mind that the relationship of bike size to fairing size is important; the larger frame-mount fairings work best on bikes of 750cc and higher (which is *not* to say they can't be mounted on smaller bikes; but as bike size and weight decrease, the fairing's adverse effect on handling becomes more pronounced).

The transition from fairing-free riding to maneuvering a bike with a frame-mounted unit is probably responsible for causing a slight apprehension in more than a few riders. The reason? The first time you make a right or left-hand turn you will realize that the fairing doesn't turn with the handlebars. This is distracting at first and could cause a problem when maneuvering at night at very slow speeds since the headlight doesn't move with the handlebars.

What can you expect to pay for this type of fairing? Prices run fairly high—from around $250 for the lower-priced, stripped models at discount prices, to over $700 for a custom unit with all the options included.

When deciding which large, frame-mounted fairing will best serve your purposes, one of the first things to determine is the availability of mounting hardware suited to your motorcycle, as not all fairings fit all bikes. Craig Vetter pioneered an inroad to making fairings nearly universal by designing mounting hardware kits for each different make and model of bike. This was a new concept that had an enormous effect on marketing. It meant dealers could stock this fairing, since they only needed one or two in stock, along with a few hardware kits. This is one of the reasons this style fairing is so popular today. But since the same fairing will mount in a slightly different fashion on every motorcycle, it is a good idea to get a look at the combination of motorcycle and fairing you have in mind. This will give you a pretty good idea of how the two go together, both visually and functionally, and will offer an opportunity to assure that the wide part of the fairing aligns with the handgrips, which will influence hand protection. It's also a good idea to examine mounting hardware for your model bike. The most desirable type of mounting hardware is designed to bolt up to mounting lugs that are now found on many of the newer model bikes. With this new method you can be assured of precise alignment as well as a good solid mount. Other common mounting methods include U-bolts and hose clamps, which will provide a completely serviceable mount, but require careful initial alignment. As it is an integral part of the fairing, mounting hardware should be regularly examined for tightness and structural integrity.

Some models offer a separate knob inside the fairing for adjusting the headlight vertically. While it's not a good idea to adjust it while riding, this is a very convenient feature. Weight of fairing and hardware isn't critical in most cases; still, any weight you can save is worthwhile. Don't forget to add any accessories to be fitted for a total weight figure.

Storage space is a major benefit of this style fairing. Two types of storage covers are available—the soft, vinyl covers that snap in place and solid, locking covers. The soft covers offer easier access, but provide less security when the bike is parked. Some models offer both a soft and locking cover, one for each side, and this seems to be a reasonable compromise. A handy feature on the soft vinyl cover is a small pocket that is accessible while riding. Probably the most important aspect of the covers, aside from locking or snap closure, is water tightness. Examine the inside edge around the opening to see if it is slightly raised; this raised portion under the cover will generally keep out water. The raised portion may be molded into the ABS frame, or be a separate piece of trim around the opening. The next thing to check is accessibility to the storage area, in addition to its volume. If electrical wiring is routed throughout the inside of the storage area, it will be less usable than if the wires are wrapped together at the bottom of the compartment. Some models offer storage that extends up into the nose of the fairing, right behind the headlight. See if you can get your arm into the opening for access to this area. If you can, the area will be usable for lightweight items, like clothing.

Check what kind of headlight the fairing uses. Is it identical to the one that is standard on your bike, or is it different? Either way is acceptable, but the important thing is to use a quartz halogen lamp. Most new bikes are now standard with this type of light and it doesn't make sense to reduce the amount of available light by using an old-style headlight by installing a fairing. If the quartz light doesn't come standard on the fairing you like, it might be available as an option; if so, figure it in as part of the cost. While quartz bulbs are generally more expensive than the automotive-style, sealed-beam replacement unit (and more difficult to find), the added light is well worth the extra cost.

If you seek maximum protection for your legs, select a fairing with standard or

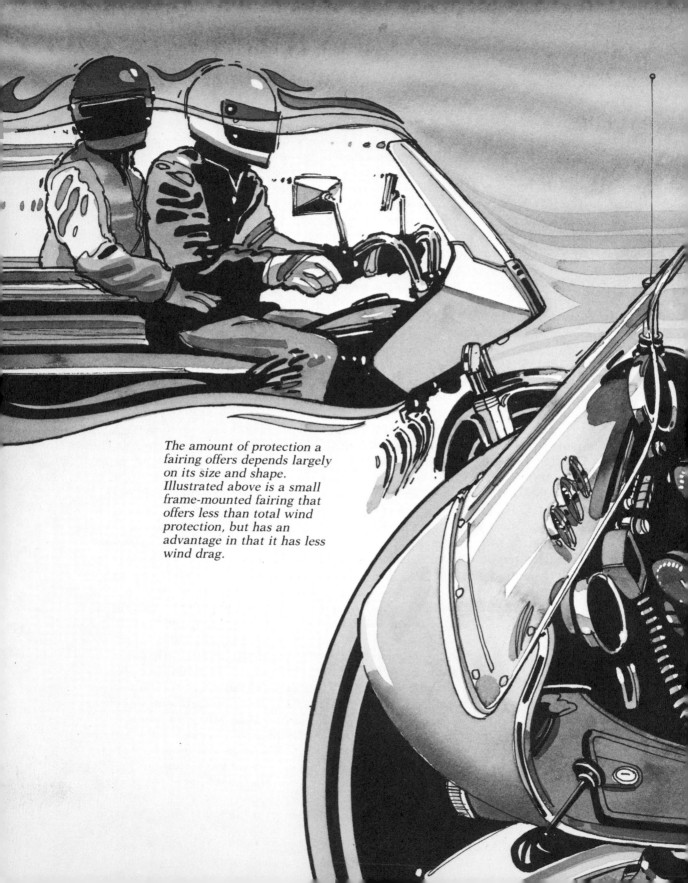

The amount of protection a fairing offers depends largely on its size and shape. Illustrated above is a small frame-mounted fairing that offers less than total wind protection, but has an advantage in that it has less wind drag.

A large frame-mounted fairing (above) places the rider and most of the passenger in a comfortable pocket of nearly still air. The more vertical the angle of the fairing, the larger the pocket of air. Larger fairings, as shown in the center illustration, provide more space for additional accessories and increased storage capacity.

optional lowers. I personally like lowers and use them on a regular basis, for the same reason I use a fairing—protection. Removable lowers are handy in cold weather, but in cold weather any ventilation is welcome. As a result, most touring riders usually leave their lowers on all the time. Ventilation can also be achieved through some form of opening or vent, but few work very well. The vents incorporated in the windshield are the least effective. Newer fairings feature vent intakes mounted low on the front of the fairing that seem to provide better ventilation, although I believe there is still room for further design improvement in this area.

Some models include provisions for numerous accessories. One of the major accessories for a frame-mounted fairing is a radio and/or tape deck. Even though these accessories will add to the weight and complexity of the wiring, some riders find it worth the cost and effort. Even if the fairing selected doesn't have radio and speaker compartments molded in, add-on radio housings are available and they do an admirable job. Auxiliary instruments are other desirable accessories, and might include clock, volt meter, and possibly an outside temperature gauge as well as oil temperature and pressure gauges. On some fairings, these will be molded in-dash; on others, they are incorporated into an add-on module. One of the most common accessories is a cigarette lighter, which offers even non-smokers a good spot for plugging in other accessories, such as a trouble light or radar detector.

The large frame-mounted fairing offers the best protection, the most features and the highest cost. A more subtle benefit of a large fairing is the image it projects about you as a rider. This fairing style appears to be associated with responsible, law-abiding riders, hence I seem to get slightly better treatment when I ride a fairing-equipped bike. It's a nebulous sort of thing, but one I am convinced is real. This style of fairing has come to be closely associated with the American touring bike for good reason—it offers many solid benefits for touring.

While the dividing line between the large and small frame-mounted fairings is somewhat indistinct, it is worth noting. The differences are related to both size and weight. The dividing line in size can be placed right around 28 inches in width; those 29 inches and over can be termed large, those 28 inches and less are small. But weight also plays a part, so a fairing must be under 25 pounds to fit the "small" definition. The smaller models are relatively new on the market, but their popularity is growing rapidly. They offer the same benefits as the larger models—protection, storage space—and some of the adverse effects, such as handling input. But they usually do not have as dramatic an effect on fuel consumption, perhaps even offering a mild improvement in this area over a bare bike. Since the main reason for installing a fairing is wind protection, the reduced protection offered by the smaller models must be considered carefully. Many fork-mounted fairings are guilty of allowing updrafts to hit a rider's face, but rarely is this type of wind felt on any frame-mounted fairing, even on small models. Where the reduced protection will be most keenly felt is on the hands, arms and shoulders. The wind will not be enough to produce any serious degree of fatigue; there is more wind buffeting, of course, and this can be tiring—but it's certainly not like riding without any protection at all. Buffeting causes an overall fatigue as opposed to

Illustrated here are two views of frame-mounted fairings—clearly showing the relationship of size to protection against wind, dust and flying debris.

the direct, muscular fatigue of holding your body against the wind all day. The major sacrifices won't be noticed, though, until cold weather is encountered, because that's when the reduced protection is most noticeable.

Many small fairings are available with optional lowers to extend protection to the lower legs. One manufacturer offers optional extenders for added hand protection. The trade-off in reduced wind protection is not as great as it might seem, however, because these small fairings do offer quite a few advantages. The major advantage is the reduced effect these lighter, smaller fairings have on handling. The combination of smaller size and lighter weight, together with the fact that it's mounted on the frame, produces a fairing with the least handling input of any touring-type wind protection. These smaller models offer most of the benefits of the larger models, like storage space and room for accessories. But don't be surprised if the smaller fairings do not sport a lower price tag than the larger fairings. Some manufacturers produce this size fairing because they feel it is the best size, and not, as you might think, to reduce the price. So it pays to check dimensions, especially overall width and total weight figures, to identify which class a particular model fits into.

The reduction in frontal area on small fairings results in reduced power requirements, and makes for easier handling than the larger models do. So this size fairing is well worth considering for nearly any size bike from 400cc and up. Small fairings are especially suited to riders who put a premium on bike handling and performance, yet want some of the protection and storage of the larger models. Prices start only slightly lower than the large models—around $200 for a stripped version at a discount price, and up to $600 for a fairing with all the optional accessories.

Fork-mounted Fairings

This style fairing represents both the oldest and the newest offerings on the fairing market. The old-style, fork-mounted fairings have a solid body of ABS plastic or fiberglass similar in look to the frame-mounted models. But fork-mounted fairings rarely offer interior storage space, because they are usually made from a single molding. The newer-style, fork-mount fairings are completely clear and usually made of plexiglass, with much less visual impact than a full fairing. In addition, they offer scant opportunity for styling innovations (such as a special paint job), and they don't increase the visual bulk of the bike, making your machine less visible to automobile drivers than a motorcycle with a full fairing. In some respects, there isn't much to distinguish a clear, fork-mounted fairing from the smaller and less expensive windshields, but there are some important differences worth examining.

The major difference between a fairing and a windshield is that fairings are considerably larger and extended in width at the handlebars for increased hand protection. Some models are also extended down along the fork tubes in order to eliminate the upward flow of air which usually plagues riders with fork-mounted fairings. These fairings also have one advantage over the full frame-mounted models—they turn with the handlebars—which means the headlights will point in the same direction as the front wheel during parking lot maneuvers. Probably the biggest advantage of fork-mount fairings is the smaller chunk they will take out of your checkbook. The clear models are priced around $100, while the older-style, fork-mount models of ABS plastic or fiberglass run from around $125 to $250.

Conversely, one disadvantage of these fairings is their effect on motorcycle handling. Anything attached to the handlebars or front forks will generate some steering input, and the fork-mounted fairings are the largest items to be attached there. While the problems don't usually start until fairly high speeds (over 70 mph or so in still air), it's impossible to ride in still air all the time. Gusty winds from any quarter other than dead ahead or astern will be felt. At normal highway speeds, around 60 mph, the effect on steering with this type of fairing will certainly be felt, but should prove completely manageable, if not especially pleasant. Probably the most common example of this steering input will occur on freeways or interstates where the big 18-wheelers create quite a bit of turbulence. But this effect is felt on any bike regardless of equipment; it's just more pronounced with a fork-mounted fairing. This style fairing offers very good protection, at least in the new, all clear versions, and the price is right, too. But you get all this at the expense of handling.

Windshields

We can put nearly all other forms of wind protection under this heading, although some windshields would be more properly called quarter fairings. In general, this

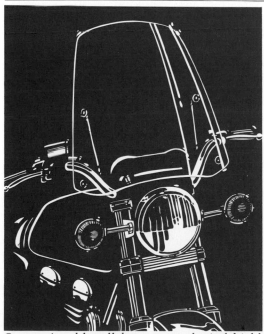

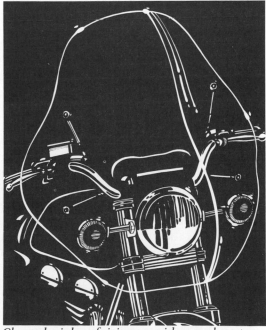

Conventional handlebar-mounted windshield offers easy installation and reasonable price.

Clear plexiglass fairing provides good protection but can affect handling in gusty winds.

category includes small fork or handlebar-mounted wind deflectors. By definition, their protection doesn't extend to the hands or arms. They range in size from the large, police-style windshields to the tiny "belly-button" pseudo-fairings seen on some racy-looking stock bikes. The larger models in this category (from about 15 to 18 inches wide and 22 to 24 inches tall) will offer fair wind protection to the body, while the smaller models offer very little protection from the chilling effects of the wind. But that doesn't mean they don't provide a useful function. Even the smallest models will help reduce wind pressure on the chest and upper body, which is fine when riding around town; but I wouldn't recommend their use for touring. They will not affect handling as greatly as a fork- or frame-mounted fairing and are priced much lower, from $50 to $100.

Luggage Systems

The traditional image of a touring bike would not be complete without a pair of saddlebags flanking the rear wheel. But saddlebags are far too functional as touring equipment to be considered just a dress-up item. Two-up riders planning anything longer than weekend jaunts will discover saddlebags are virtually mandatory. With a passenger taking up the back half of the seat, there is not much room to carry the gear needed by two people for extended touring. (For a full discussion of loading and packing, see Chapter 9.) Even the solo touring rider, with less to carry and more room to carry it, will find saddlebags offer convenience and security, as well as numerous other advantages.

The three major categories of saddlebags include hard-bodied, detachable; hard-bodied, permanently-mounted; and soft-bodied, detachable types. Each type will be dealt with separately, but there are a number of benefits they all have in common. First, they all utilize an otherwise unusable space on the bike—the area on either side of the rear wheel below seat level. Although this spot is not the perfect location for carrying added weight, it's still one of the better locations. Second, while few saddlebags are totally watertight, they do offer quite a bit of protection from dirt and water. All it takes to keep your clothes and camping gear perfectly dry in the worst of storms is a large plastic trash bag. A plastic bag will self-destruct unprotected on the back of a bike in the wind, but inside a saddlebag it will turn the leakiest models into little islands of dryness. In general, saddlebags offer secure storage—security from being lost or falling off the bike in transit as well as security from theft. While the solid bags offer the most theft security, the soft bags offer nearly as much protection if they are not obviously detachable. Most passengers seem to like the feeling of personal security the bags offer, as the bulk of the bags, out to each side, gives more visual substance to their seating position. Saddlebags have a minimum effect on handling; their effect on the motorcycle seems to be directly related to how much they weigh and how they are mounted. One manufacturer has developed a flexible mount for their hard-bodied bags that reduces the effect on handling when the bags are fully loaded. By their nature, soft throw-over saddlebags achieve a slight movement independent of the bike, which lessens their effect on handling. There is some evidence that a fairing-equipped bike will suffer from slightly less aerodynamic drag when equipped with saddlebags. In actual practice, I haven't been able to detect any differences in fuel consumption one way or the other with saddlebags.

The style of saddlebags you choose will probably be governed by aesthetic considerations, which is fine if they also offer the functional capabilities you require. Regardless of which style you choose, there are some general considerations to keep in mind when comparing saddlebags. A couple of things to look at rather critically are the overall width of the bags when mounted on the bike and the total weight of bags and hardware. About the only time overall width will cause any kind of problem is when it gets much wider than the handlebars or fairing. Most bars on U.S.-style touring bikes measure from 29 to about 35 inches wide, with the large, frame-mounted fairings running about the same width. Exceeding this width with a set of saddlebags isn't going to cause any major problems, but it could be an annoyance. Bags wider than the fairing or bars tend to get in the way in tight maneuvers such as pulling into parking spaces. If the widest point on the bike is behind me, I tend to misjudge how much space I need.

Overall weight is a more important consideration, especially for two-up riders. Every pound added in the form of bags and mounting hardware will eat into the load capacity remaining for actual touring gear. The range of total weight for solid-bodied bags is quite large, from 15 pounds to around 50 pounds. The difference of 35 pounds between the lightest and the heaviest could represent everything a touring couple might carry in a set of saddlebags. While overall width and weight might appear to be a trade-off with capacity, the relationship is not nearly as direct as it would seem. Many of the widest and heaviest bags do not offer the greatest capacity. Cubic capacity is a little difficult to determine, in some instances, because looks can be deceiving—as can some manufacturers' claims. When considering usable capacity, the shape of the saddlebags will have considerable bearing. A plain, rectangular shape is the easiest to pack and figuring cubic capacity is fairly simple. In this case, width multiplied by depth multiplied by length equals cubic capacity in inches. Unfortunately, few saddlebags are rectangular, but if you are willing to go to some bother you can measure the cubic capacity of any shape saddlebag. Fill the saddlebag with styrofoam packing chips and dump them into a cardboard box. If the lid offers some capacity, fill it with chips and pour them on top of the first bunch in the box. Now, simply multiply length and width of the box, plus the depth of the chips, and you have approximate cubic capacity.

Like everything else, selecting the right set of saddlebags is a matter of evaluating your needs and matching them with what looks good to you and fits the limitations of your particular bike and style of touring.

Hard-bodied, Detachable Saddlebags

In the mid-1970s, German-made Krauser saddlebags were introduced to the American touring market. Mike Krauser, a contemporary of fairing designer Craig Vetter, saw a need for "something better" as a result of his own motorcycle touring and proceeded to design and build it. As a result, we have the detachable, suitcase-style saddlebags characterized by their top-mounted handle, quick detachability and side loading capabilities. In many respects, these are the most convenient bags to use. The detachable feature allows very convenient and civilized loading and unloading on a bed or table indoors or at a campsite and eliminates the packrat style of loading and unloading required with some bags, where one must make repeated trips back and forth to the bike. The large lid on this style bag makes finding everything in the bag relatively easy, but the side-opening feature does require getting used to when opening it on the bike. I find it's perfectly natural to catch the lid with a knee when I'm getting into this type of bag while it's on the bike. This way things don't come cascading out of the bag onto the ground. In general, these bags offer the greatest capacity, with moderate weight and width on the bike. One problem they do have shows up when they are dirty with road grime. If taken indoors they will shed some of this dirt on anything they come in contact with. Since they are easily detached, it means the bike can be used without the bags, but with the hardware left in place.

These bags are not for everyone. I'm certain some riders find their extremely functional design a bit distracting from the bike's overall appearance. A few saddlebag manufacturers have made these bags more appealing by color-matching them to the most popular motorcycle colors and by downplaying the suitcase look. Anyone who believes that "form follows function" should have little trouble adapting to the original style that makes no attempt to disguise its suitcase heritage. The various styling changes meant to appeal to a rider's sense of aesthetics do not seriously detract from the bag's many functional virtues, although it does tend to reduce the ease of packing somewhat. Prices start around $200 and run as high as $400 per set, which makes these bags the most expensive of the luggage systems, but they are also the most versatile.

Hard-bodied, Non-detachable Saddlebags

For many riders, the permanently-mounted saddlebag is the only style that "looks right" for touring. A good part of this attitude can be traced to the fact that Harley-Davidson has been installing this style saddlebag on its big touring bikes since the early 1950s, so many American riders grew up seeing this type of saddlebag on touring motorcycles. Part of this traditional look can also be attributed to the customizing possibilities offered by this style bag. Many models are available with standard or optional chrome guard bars around the outside of the saddlebags. These guard bars have to be treated pretty much as window dressing, for while they do protect the saddlebags in a fall, the chrome will be more difficult and/or more expensive to repair than the saddlebag it's protecting. These metal guard bars add an appreciable amount of weight, and bags that incorporate them are usually among the very heaviest models.

In addition to their traditional looks, this style bag offers top loading. This pretty well eliminates the problem of contents spilling out when the bag is opened, and it also takes quite a bit of searching to find anything near the bottom of the bag. Numerous trips to the bike are required when packing and unpacking, although the introduction of soft, removable inner bags has improved this situation. Of course, riders can add their own soft inner bags to nearly any saddlebag. Not all saddlebags of this style will work with the inner bag (unless the opening of the inner bag is smaller than the saddlebag opening.) When they do work, they are a big improvement. The water-repellant inner bag has many of the virtues of the detachable-style saddlebags, but retains all the features to be found in the permanent-mounted style. The inner bag stays cleaner when in use than the exterior of the detachable bag, and it does a reasonably good job of keeping the contents dry in heavy rains. The inner bag can also be carried into your motel room or tent, and, since the saddlebags are still attached to the bike, you are free to make a run to the grocery store or restaurant, using the empty saddlebags for carrying packages or storing your jacket, gloves and helmet. Not all saddlebags are large enough to hold a helmet or accommodate the soft inner bags, so be sure to investigate the options available. The inner bags have effectively eliminated one of the major disadvantages of this popular style touring luggage, and I would strongly recommend including them. Prices for the non-detachable saddlebags range from $150 to $300.

Soft-bodied, Throw-over Bags

Probably the oldest style saddlebag made, the original throw-over saddlebags were made for camels, then horses, so they have been around for a long, long time. The earliest motorcycle saddlebags were made of leather (soft-bodied) and attached permanently to the motorcycle. A few of this style are still available from European manufacturers, although they are less common now than the throw-over style bags. Instead, the market has gone to some thoroughly modern designs made from high-quality materials offering fairly good storage capacity and some unique advantages. These are by far the lightest saddlebags available, because they require no mounting hardware, and are made of heavy-duty fabric instead of ABS plastic or fiberglass. The common mode of attachment is to lay the saddlebags across the seat and to secure them with some form of tie-down or strap. Some models also have connecting straps underneath the seat, but in practice the tie-downs aren't really necessary. This style is most appealing to riders who like a bare bike when they aren't touring, because the bags are so easily removed and stored. The storage capacity will be less than the large, detachable style bag, but they offer easy portability to and from the bike. Several of the newer throw-over bags are equipped with extra loops of webbing at the top edge, so when two bags are carried together, the two loops come together to form a very effective handle for carrying the bags off the bike. Water repellency varies, but none are completely watertight. A plastic bag is still a necessity if you want dry clothes. These bags are especially appropriate for solo touring, where a single rider can get by with the reduced luggage capacity. By virtue of their light weight, they make an excellent choice for the touring rider who opts for a smaller motorcycle, and they are appropriate also for two-up riders facing strict weight limitations.

The throw-over style adapts well to the Custom or Special bikes, proving to be more suited to the bike's design, which usually incorporates short, upswept exhaust pipes that hamper the use of the more traditional, hard-bodied saddlebags. These bags make a good choice for those who trade bikes frequently; since they don't actually

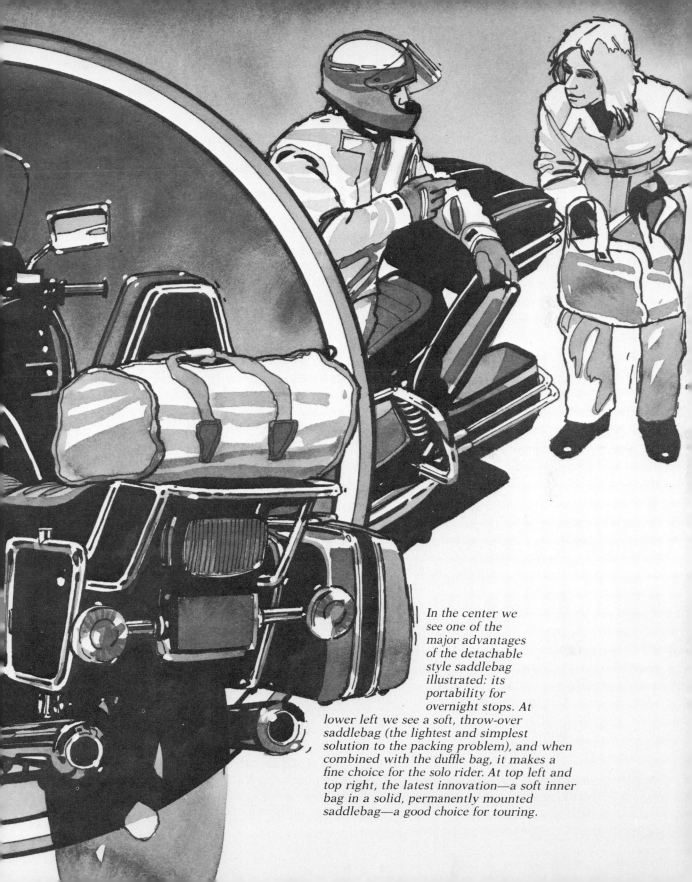

In the center we see one of the major advantages of the detachable style saddlebag illustrated: its portability for overnight stops. At lower left we see a soft, throw-over saddlebag (the lightest and simplest solution to the packing problem), and when combined with the duffle bag, it makes a fine choice for the solo rider. At top left and top right, the latest innovation—a soft inner bag in a solid, permanently mounted saddlebag—a good choice for touring.

mount on the bike, they can be used with any model. Pricewise, this choice is the least expensive way to get the added luggage capacity of saddlebags. Prices will run from a low of around $40 up to $150.

Soft Luggage

Strictly speaking, soft luggage doesn't fall into the motorcycle accessory category, since certain items like duffle bags and backpacks can be so easily detached and used for other purposes off the bike. But one item that I consider the best piece of luggage a touring rider can own is the tank bag, and it definitely falls into the category of touring-related accessories. I say "best" because the location a tank bag occupies is the ideal spot for packing extra weight. But a tank bag offers numerous other benefits as well, such as the security of its contents. Nearly everything carried on a touring motorcycle is packed out of sight behind the rider (except the storage in the fairing) and if something should come loose or break open, it can be some time before the rider is aware of it. By that time, and I speak from experience, your possessions can be strung out along the road for miles. I had an experience once with a set of prototype side-loading saddlebags, and the door came open without my realizing it. I was able to retrieve all but my checkbook, which was found several weeks later by a highway construction worker. For this reason, I now carry cameras, checkbook, money, credit cards and other valuables in a tank bag in front of me. Tank bags are easily removed from the bike, and can be taken with you if there is any question about security when the bike is parked. A tank bag is truly worth the purchase, if for no other reason than to utilize the see-through plastic map holder. I like to know where I am all the time— I might not know just where I'm going, but I like to know what my options are. The tank bag is easily accessible, and with some forethought, everything you need for a day's ride can be packed in the tank bag or the fairing storage pockets.

The medium-sized tank bag has worked best for me; it is a comfortable size to carry loaded, yet large enough to offer real storage capacity. Look for a bag that is 12 to 15 inches long, 10 to 12 inches wide and from 8 to 12 inches deep. Some models have several pockets, in addition to a large central compartment which allows you to separate small items into easy-to-find pockets. If the bag you select has only one large compartment, you can achieve the same effect by purchasing two or three lightweight nylon, backpacker belt pouches with a zippered top opening. These pouches can be used to separate small items in the bag, especially if you choose different colors for telling them apart. A 1,200 to 1,500 cubic-inch capacity is large enough for all-around use, but be certain the map pocket on the top is at least nine inches wide, so that oil company maps will fit comfortably.

Tank bags are made from a variety of materials, but I especially favor the urethane-backed Cordura nylon, with Naugahyde vinyl my second choice for a good-looking, serviceable bag. Prices for this type and size tank bag will run from around $40 to $75; smaller and larger bags will be priced correspondingly lower or higher. Don't let a tank bag's unusual appearance put you off; they are easy to get used to and rarely interfere with your riding. The only time tank bags get in the way is during parking lot maneuvers, where the handlebars are turned all the way and the grips bump into the bag. (Don't be surprised when this causes the horn to honk!) Another negative aspect of tank bags is the necessity of removing them to gas up, but this turns out to be a minor price to pay for the convenience they offer. Most tank bags are designed to make gassing up a simple, one-step procedure. There is some slight chance of scratching the paint on the gas tank, but most manufacturers take great pains to guard against it. If there should be an exposed buckle or piece of metal that might rub the tank, a little plastic electrical tape will cover it and protect your paint job.

If, for some reason, I had to select a single accessory for touring and could use no other, I would pick the biggest tank bag I could find. I could carry all my touring gear in it, if I packed very light; a tank bag would offer a fair degree of wind protection, and I would always know where everything was while I was riding. I wouldn't have to worry about things flying off the back, and the tank bag would have almost no effect on the bike's handling. To say that I highly recommend tank bags for touring is putting it mildly.

Duffle Bags

The tank bag is a fairly specialized piece of motorcycle gear. On the other end of the luggage spectrum is the duffle bag, one of the best general purpose items you can buy. Duffle bags are available in sporting goods stores, army surplus stores and just about anywhere else where sporting equipment is sold. When I tour solo, I place the duffle bag close behind me on the seat and use it as a back rest. This also has the advantage of placing the weight as far ahead of the rear axle as possible. Two-up riders could strap a duffle on the luggage rack and use it for storing items that are too tall or too bulky for the saddlebags. Duffle bags come in all sizes, from moderate to extra-large, and are priced from seven dollars up to $75 for the deluxe versions. I carry a duffle crosswise on the motorcycle and secure it with two long bungee cords, placed through the handles and hooked on either side of the bike. This mode of attachment is quick and easy and allows the bag to move slightly so that it exerts less effect on the bike's handling.

When selecting a duffle bag for touring, there are a number of points to consider. Duffle bags designed for boaters come the closest to being waterproof. A greater degree of water repellency is assured if the zipper is covered with a flap of material that fastens down with Velcro or snaps. Duffle fabrics range from lightweight nylon and cotton duck material, in the less expensive models, to high quality, urethane-backed Cordura nylon. As with tank bags and outer garments, a good application of water repellant spray will help keep the bags cleaner and the contents dryer, regardless of fabric. The original Army duffles opened from the top, but are less convenient than the modern versions, which feature a full-length zipper that runs from end to end. This offers easier packing and better access. Nylon coil zippers are the most water repellant and expensive, but good brass zippers are quite satisfactory. The zipper is usually the first thing to go on duffle bags, so pay close attention to its quality at the time of purchase. Some duffle bags offer smaller side or end pockets, which are handy for segregating small items from the rest of the contents, and making them more accessible. There are a number of special-purpose, soft carrying cases on the market today, but the duffle bag works best for general use.

Luggage Racks

Probably the most common accessory seen on motorcycles is the luggage rack, and it is quite desirable—especially so for two-up touring. Mounting hardware for many of the hard-bodied saddlebags will include a luggage rack, at least as an optional item. The racks incorporated into saddlebag mounting hardware will add the least weight. The first consideration for a luggage rack is that it be mounted as low and as close to the back of the seat as possible. Nearly any style luggage rack will be satisfactory, as long as it is made of sturdy materials. A broken rack is worse than no rack at all and

A luggage rack is especially appreciated by the two-up rider, as seating space that would be available for carrying equipment is lost. Remember that most luggage racks are not designed to carry heavy loads, and, generally, the shorter and lower the rack, the better for riding stability.

is generally a pain in the schedule. Don't neglect weight considerations; a couple of pounds saved adds up in the end.

Backpacks

While backpacks are wonders of modern engineering and construction, they are less than ideal for touring—unless backpacking is to be a part of your touring agenda. In that case, the internal frame packs are best, as they are smaller and offer more interior space than most of the external frame packs. Regardless of what type of luggage you use, the major concern is keeping the weight close to the rider or passenger and as low as possible.

Travel Trunks

A travel trunk is basically a plastic or fiberglass box that bolts to the luggage rack. Trunks are found on a great many touring bikes, but I have to admit to a strong prejudice against them. I feel they put weight in the very worst position and have an exaggerated effect on handling. They can be a handy and secure place to store helmets, jackets and gloves, and passengers appreciate the backrest and accompanying sense of personal security. If you find a travel trunk to be a necessity, I would suggest keeping it empty while traveling and using it only when the bike is parked. I have used them for many thousands of miles on test bikes and can understand why many riders like them, but it hasn't changed my opinion of them. There are better options for touring. An exception is a new model that sits on top of the passenger portion of the seat, which keeps it up over the axle, rather than out behind it. But even with this improvement, I think a good duffle bag does just as good a job, if not better.

Suspension Components

Motorcycle manufacturers have started taking steps to solve the suspension problems touring riders have faced for years. The problem is primarily one of versatility, or rather lack of versatility, in the suspension—especially at the rear. A bare bike, ridden solo, might place 290 pounds on the rear suspension, a reasonably accurate figure for the weight capacity of the majority of large bikes on the market today. But a bike, fully loaded for touring and equipped with a full complement of accessories and passenger, might place a burden of nearly 700 pounds on the rear. That represents a 140-percent weight increase; almost the same as if you placed 2,000 pounds of extra weight in the back seat of a 4,000-pound automobile that already has 1,500 pounds of car weight on the rear axle. The rear bumper of the car would probably drag on the pavement; at least the motorcycle will still function with this kind of weight, but this should illustrate the scope of the problem.

If the bike manufacturer selects springs to handle the maximum load possible, the solo rider with a bare motorcycle will have so little suspension movement at the rear that it might as well not be there. But if the suspension is designed for the minimum load, the touring rider is left with his tail dragging. Obviously, a compromise is selected, but with a steel spring it is still not possible to make the suspension work properly at both extremes. This is where air springs come into the picture. They are commonly called "air shocks," but actually they are a regular hydraulic shock incorporated into the air springs. The latest models are not only air-adjustable springs, but allow for adjusting the damping of the shocks with external control. Air springs allow the rider to select the appropriate air pressure for proper ride height, handling precision and ride for a given load. The newest motorcycles are showing up with both front and rear air suspension, although front air forks are still more common than rear air springs. Older bikes that lack air forks can be retrofitted with air caps for front forks. Air springs will help regain lost ride height and suspension travel lost at the front from the addition of accessories and touring load, and they do wonders for the loaded touring bike when installed on the rear. The adjustability of air is the big factor; it allows the rider to firm up the rear suspension so that the bike is much more manageable with a load. A bike fitted with air shocks will regain most of the cornering clearance lost from added weight, as well as offer a decent ride over big bumps where the overloaded original equipment rear suspension would bottom out easily. Air suspension isn't a license to overload indiscriminantly, although it will contribute to safety, comfort and riding pleasure.

Accessory air springs for the rear run around $150 a set. They are relatively simple to install, but allow yourself about a half day to do the job correctly. One manufacturer offers an onboard air compressor and remote controls, including air gauges, so that air suspension at one or both ends can be adjusted while riding. Now *that's* versatility! This optional setup is quite expensive—around $300—but it offers the ultimate in allowing the rider to not only adjust for load, but for road condition and type of road, whether curving mountain passes or interstate highways. Two-up touring riders who ride solo around town are going to derive the most benefit from adjustable air suspension, but nearly any touring rider will appreciate its advantages.

Custom Seats

A great many accessories, such as air springs, are designed to correct a particular fault in a particular motorcycle destined to be a touring bike. One of the most common complaints of any motorcycle rider concerns uncomfortable seats. Believe me, the wrong motorcycle seat can become incredibly uncomfortable. Motorcycle manufacturers are making some progress in the improvement of seat comfort, but the very best seats are those made by quality custom seat manufacturers. Don't rush out and purchase a custom seat unless you are certain the stock model is totally unsuitable. Even the best seat is going to feel uncomfortable the first day in the saddle, because your posterior will be unaccustomed to sitting on a bike for such a long period of time. Discomfort is one thing—pain is an entirely different matter. Some seats become so uncomfortable they cause acute pain. In such cases, some type of remedy is definitely called for. Budget allowing, a custom seat is the best choice, and will cost you from $150 to $300. Selection of a custom seat is not a frivolous affair. Some seats are sold on an exchange basis; you exchange your stock seat plus cash for the new seat. These manufacturers use stock seat pans to build their custom seats, and they generally provide the best fit and most reliability. Sit on the seat you are selecting when it is installed on a motorcycle—does it put you in a natural and relaxed position for riding, and feel comfortable? Then it probably will work fine. Check that the area at the inner thighs doesn't create much pressure when your feet are on the pegs. The double bucket seat usually works best for two-up riders. Examine the stitching and the way the underside has been finished; careful workmanship usually indicates a quality seat. If your budget can't stand the strain of a full-fledged custom job, there are some ways to overcome a painful seat. One fairly inexpensive method of posterior protection is a water or air-filled seat cover. Both work well and will appreciably improve seating comfort. On the road, if you just need a quick remedy, a one-half to three-quarter-inch-thick piece of foam rubber wide enough to cover the seat and held down by your body weight, will help considerably.

Other Accessories

Handlebars and handgrips are among the other items that can be adjusted to make your motorcycle better suited to your particular anatomy. The handlebars can be bent slightly for a more comfortable riding position, especially if they feel too wide or cause you to lean too far forward. To adjust the handlebars, place the bike on the stand, swing the bars over to full lock and then bend them a tiny bit farther—first one side, then the other. This should be done in very small increments, as a little adjustment goes a long way. If manual adjustment isn't adequate, custom handle bars are available, but be sure you know what you want before making a change. Custom handgrips are available, but I have never found the need to change handgrips, mostly because I always wear gloves. This is the best way to assure hand comfort, and gloves provide a safety measure against abrasion that custom grips can't provide.

Horns and lights are other items that can frequently be improved upon. Quartz replacement lights will offer better nighttime visibility by increasing available light. Auxiliary lights are available, but if you don't have a specific need, I would stay away from them. They add weight and battery drain. If you regularly ride after dark in areas where animals on the road are fairly common, by all means go to the additional lights, but it might be better to merely slow down, which extends your visibility by reducing stopping distances. The stock horns on some motorcycles are a joke. If you find yourself with one of these, there are any number of alternative selections available. After trying most types, I have discovered that a good, loud pair of electric horns are the best choice. They are easy to install and are less troublesome than the more "romantic" air horns.

For safety reasons, I take a rather dim view of a couple of items that are listed as touring comfort accessories—namely, floorboards and highway pegs. When floorboards are used, the foot must be lifted to apply the rear brake; only a fraction of a second is lost in doing this, but it could be a crucial fraction of a second. Some riders find them more comfortable for long rides, but an alternative solution for uncomfortable feet might be to try heavier boots or a different style of footwear. Boots are available that are specifically designed for riding and have small rubber fins between heel and sole, right where the peg rides most of the time, that spread the pressure out over a wider area and are considerably more comfortable for long-distance riding. As for highway pegs, I'll grant that they relieve the discomfort that can develop from keeping your legs in the same position for long periods of time. But it's a simple matter to stretch your legs out to the side or ahead momentarily to accomplish essentially the same thing. Riding with feet up on highway pegs puts the rider way out of position to respond to any kind of an emergency, whether it's a sudden traffic jam, a dog or cat running out into the road or a flat tire. I don't recommend them. The right accessories are an important part of the right bike for touring. It's like the mechanic who has to use a big pair of channel-lock pliers when all he needs is a one-quarter-inch box end wrench. It's just a matter of suitability.

Chapter 5
What to Wear

Your introduction to "riding apparel" probably was presented in a doomsday, after-the-fact manner, i.e., "When you go down," or "If you have an accident . . ." Although accurate, this is not the whole story regarding clothing and safety.

The first function of clothing is physical comfort, which is inseparable from safe riding. I wonder about the bootless, helmetless, jacketless rider whose attention should be centered on the road—on that car making an illegal left turn—when in reality his attention is centered on the left ankle which has been struck by a sharp rock at 60 mph or a bee that got into his sleeve.

In almost all cases, dressing with forethought constitutes the ounce of prevention that keeps "the shiny side up." Dressing for the road is serious business, especially for the touring rider who, in a single week-long trip, may encounter every sort of weather condition imaginable. Proper clothing ensures that a motorcycle excursion needn't be Chinese torture or an endurance test. Instead, you have the freedom (there's that word again) to experience nature at her best (and her worst) and still come out smiling, with stories to tell afterward that sound more like John Muir than Alfred Hitchcock. "Remember that trip to Yellowstone where we had two days of rain followed by the hail and snowstorm . . . Wow! . . . What a trip!" Long-distance touring riders, as opposed to daily commuters or weekend dabblers, are especially vulnerable to the weather, because while they're on the road the bike is their sole form of transportation. There is no comfortable station wagon in which to do the shopping or run to the bank, should the weather suddenly turn nasty.

While safety and comfort are closely related, there is another important factor. Long before safety is seriously affected, one's enjoyment of riding and seeing new country may be diminished. I recall an evening ride across the desert toward Las Vegas. It was late fall and the wind had become quite chilly by the time the sun had set an hour ago. I was feeling chilled, but hadn't bothered to stop and add clothing until I realized I was really getting uncomfortable. I pulled over and added a layer or two of protection (it only took a couple of minutes) and resumed the ride. Suddenly, it seemed the desert sky was ablaze with stars. It was a magnificent night to be out riding and

I realized the beauty had been there all the time. I just hadn't noticed until I had regained the physical comfort which allowed me to fully appreciate it. When a rider is uncomfortable, beautiful scenery loses much or most of its impact.

Some riders may ask, isn't discomfort part of touring on a motorcycle? And the answer is: only if you allow it to be. It is possible to carry a set of clothing on a bike that will offer protection and comfort from around zero degrees to over 100 degrees F., whether it's raining or the sun is shining. By selecting the right garments, this set of clothing will offer the needed weather-and-accident protection; more, it will be compact for packing and suitable for activities off the bike. Compactness will be especially important for two-up riders, where weight and space limitations require careful selection of everything to be carried.

Part of this comfort thing goes back to why we tour. If the purpose is to enjoy ourselves, to see new country, enjoy riding and experience adventure, a fair degree of physical comfort doesn't seem out of place. Most of us are far more inclined to go for a one-day ride only when the weather is nice, mainly because it's more fun and comfortable. But when we go touring, we take the days as they come. The best way to make every day comfortable and fun is through proper dress. When we are comfortable, the mind doesn't dwell on it. We just *are.* But if we are uncomfortable, the mind can't leave it alone—and as the discomfort grows, so does the amount of attention we pay to it. The word "discomfort" is simply another way of saying "mild pain." If discomfort is carried far enough, it becomes pain. I don't know of anyone who goes touring because it's painful—even mildly. Proper dress must take into consideration all the different aspects of protection a rider's body requires for motorcycle riding.

What kind of protection can clothing provide? Obviously, the primary protection is doomsday attire. In the event of an accident or spill, the right clothing will help. If the accident is minor, it will help greatly in keeping the damage minor.

The major item in this category is a helmet. While its life-saving aspects are real, it does offer other benefits. Two basic helmet styles are offered. The three-quarter style leaves the face open, while the full-face model adds jaw protection. The old one-half style, favored for so many years by police officers, is being phased out. Even policemen are on the way to wearing models that offer the best protection. And while that protection is the primary reason for wearing a helmet, it does offer other benefits, like keeping your head warm. It even keeps long hair from becoming a mass of tangles. If a major accident occurs, your dress (including your helmet), may save your life.

I rode motorcycles long before helmets were in common use, much less available, but now I find touring less tiring when I wear a helmet, mainly through the reduction of wind noise and buffeting. For many years, I favored the three-quarter helmet because I enjoyed the "wind-in-the-face" feel of riding with only my eyes covered by glass or plastic. A fairing or windscreen also contributed to the deflection of the wind and/or various unidentified airborne objects. Recently, though, I have switched to the full-coverage helmet because I appreciate the additional protection for the chin and face that this model offers. But I tend to remove the face shield except in rain or very cold weather, thus retaining some of that wind-in-the-face feeling without giving up protection.

The next consideration is abrasion protection—not one of the more pleasant aspects of riding, but certainly one that cannot be ignored. Wearing clothes for abrasion protection, along with a helmet, puts me in mind of a true story. Some years back, before seat belts were common in cars, a close friend installed them in his car. He had his mother-in-law in the back seat after picking her up at the airport for her annual visit. When she noticed the seat belts (the first she had ever seen), she asked what they were. He explained they were for protection in the event of an accident. She pondered that for some time, then asked, "But is there time to put them on?"

Seat belts, like protective clothing, must be worn *all* the time. There just isn't time to put them on when they are needed. Leather is a traditional favorite for motorcycle riding, and for good reason. It does the job where abrasion is concerned, and it also offers protection from flying objects, insects and the bits of debris that are kicked up by other vehicles.

One of the advantages of leather is that it breathes—deerskin is probably the most "breathable" of leathers available in clothing suitable for riding. Goatskin is another good leather for riding apparel, but, like deerskin, it's expensive and available in limited quantities. The most common leather used in motorcycle clothing is cowhide. It's not as breathable as deerskin or goatskin, but it's still a fine choice. This breathable quality is why leather has a reputation with some riders for not being very warm. But if you use leather as an outer layer in mild weather, and as an intermediate layer for cold or rain, it emerges as the all-around winner in riding wear.

For instance, in warm to hot weather, unlined leather gloves and a leather jacket are quite comfortable when riding, especially if only a cotton T-shirt is worn under the jacket. As soon as one steps off the bike, the gloves, jacket and helmet are removed, leaving the rider dressed comfortably for the temperature.

Leather is just as appropriate for the feet and legs. Boots, of course, are the simple answer for the feet, ankles and lower legs (especially the shins, which are sensitive and vulnerable to flying debris). But what about leather pants? They do offer good protection and I have worn them for years, but they present problems for touring. They tend to be bulky when packed and are too hot for continuous wear. For years I carried jeans and leather pants, which meant I had to find a rest room or some other place to change when the temperature required it. Later, I switched to leather chaps, and to this day I find that they offer a number of advantages. They fit perfectly with the basic concept of adding or removing clothing items rather than changing them. In hot weather at a fuel stop, the chaps are simply zipped off along with the jacket, gloves and helmet. Like these garments, the chaps can be donned or removed anywhere. Now almost the entire body can benefit from the protection of leather.

The human body has an incredibly sensitive thermostat: most people can detect a two- or three-degree difference in temperature. This is the big reason I repeatedly refer to adjustability as being desirable. On the road, I find it both comfortable and satisfying to be able to select a combination of clothing that precisely matches the temperature requirements at the moment. This doesn't mean stopping every few minutes to add or remove clothing, but it does mean there are several options besides taking just one big, heavy suit that may be too hot to wear in warm weather but necessary for the cold. Touring means preparing for the worst possible conditions and temperatures. It needn't mean a great load of clothes, but merely selecting the proper ones. As pointed out previously, discomfort is closely tied to safety in more ways than one. The first to go as a result of discomfort is your enjoyment of the scenery. Then your attention is distracted from traffic conditions, road surface, etc.

While all of the above protections are real and important, the condition that causes most riders the most concern is riding in cold and rain. Heat can be a problem, but it's generally more endurable than cold and you don't run the risk of a dangerous side effect of prolonged exposure to cold and damp—hypothermia. The extreme result of hypothermia is unconsciousness or death, but it can be avoided if you are aware of the warning signals before it becomes too advanced. Hypothermia is defined as "subnormal temperature of the body" and mainly refers to the core temperature in the trunk of the body. One of the early signs of hypothermia is uncontrolled shivering, but there is an even more dangerous symptom—loss of ability to make rational decisions. Allowing yourself to remain uncomfortable in the cold is not only unpleasant but dangerous. Contributing greatly to hypothermia is wind chill, which quickly lowers the core temperature, even on fairly warm days.

Actually, it's probably redundant to outline why one should keep the body warm on a bike, as anyone with riding experience knows the seat of a motorcycle can be one of the coldest places on earth. The inexperienced rider is apt to overcompensate after one or two teeth-chattering experiences by rushing out to buy the biggest, warmest garment he can find. While this is understandable and acceptable for the local or commuting rider, it has serious drawbacks for the touring rider. If we rephrase the new rider's vow from "stay warm, no matter what," to one that calls for keeping the body "comfortable, no matter what," it's just another way of saying essentially the same thing, but it will still help to clarify the approach outlined here. A touring rider's clothing should allow him to adjust to the conditions, regardless of what they are. The new rider may ask, "Ah, who needs warm clothing for touring in the middle of the summer?" I helped one such rider with the loan of warmer riding clothes in the middle of a snowstorm in the Rocky Mountains during July! This is not an especially common occurrence, but it does happen. Being prepared for the worst simply goes along with the basic premise of motorcycle touring—that of being self-sufficient.

A good way to select clothing for cold weather is to predict the coldest temperature you can possibly encounter during a particular trip and use that as a starting point. It's far better to err on the cold side, because errors in that direction only mean a little extra bulk to pack, while in the other direction lies discomfort and reduction of enjoyment because you weren't equipped to handle the situation. Among the factors to consider in deciding what temperatures you will need to dress for are the time of year, geographical location, elevation and personal riding habits. Time of year and geographical location are straightforward. For instance, a spring ride in New England will present a different set of conditions than a summer ride in the southeastern states. Elevation is more subtle, especially in the Rocky Mountains where conditions and temperatures can fluctuate a great deal. While snowstorms in July are rare, overnight lows that dip into the 30s and 40s are common even during summer months.

Riding habits will play a big part in dress, especially in the mountains. Riders who like to get an early start or ride late in the day can expect colder temperatures than riders who only roll during the middle of the day. They start after the sun is well up and select a campsite or motel long before dark.

As children, we learned something about how to dress for the weather. At first, our parents would dress us for the outside temperature. Then as we grew older we took on more and more of the responsibility, but would still get reminders like, "Wear your jacket, it's cold out today!" or "Be sure to take your raincoat and overshoes," usually answered by "Aw, mom, do I hafta?" As adults, it's not something we think much about, unless we move to a different part of the country where an adjustment to new weather conditions is required. In many respects, this is what takes place when one starts to ride a motorcycle. Suddenly, it's a whole new world. You spent years learning how to dress and now you have to forget most of what you learned. A few activities are somewhat similar, like duck hunting, or skiing, but nothing is quite like dressing to ride a motorcycle. The combination of sitting still in a 60-mile-per-hour wind, in all sorts of weather, is literally foreign to us. Yet we've all had a taste of what we're facing when we've spent a long period of time sitting outside in cool weather. A sweater keeps the chill off, but then a cold breeze comes up and cuts right through the sweater. So we add a light windbreaker and we're comfortable. This is the principle utilized for nearly any form of cold weather dress and it goes double for motorcycling due to the constant blast of the wind—which calls for a windproof outer layer backed by an insulating layer appropriate for the temperature.

What makes all of this rather tricky for the new rider is that it's just not obvious when you are standing beside the bike. It's a warm summer evening and you are dressed comfortably for the weather—so it's difficult to appreciate that you may be freezing your tail off just a few miles down the road. Dressing comfortably requires relating current temperature to "relative" temperature while riding. Unfortunately, it's not a parallel relationship. In other words, when it's hot, there will be very little difference in comfort while stopped or riding—in the same clothes. As the actual temperature drops a little, the relative riding temperature drops a little faster. As the actual temperature keeps falling, the relative riding temperature drops *much* faster. The new rider must learn this relationship between actual temperature and relative riding temperature to select the right degree of dress for a given set of conditions. A wind chill factor chart could help somewhat, although it's not totally applicable to our needs because it deals with exposed skin.

Possibly more useful is the graph showing actual temperature vs. relative riding temperature. By using this relative riding temperature chart, a rider will have some idea how to dress for a given actual temperature. To use it, simply find the current temperature on the left, then read across and find the range of relative riding temper-

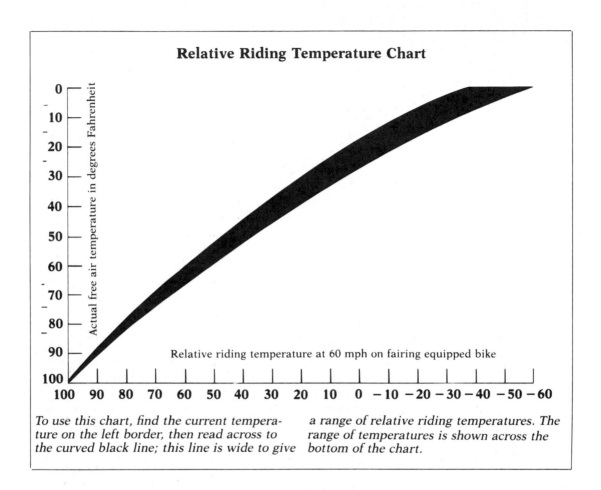

Relative Riding Temperature Chart

Actual free air temperature in degrees Fahrenheit

Relative riding temperature at 60 mph on fairing equipped bike

To use this chart, find the current tempera-ture on the left border, then read across to the curved black line; this line is wide to give *a range of relative riding temperatures. The range of temperatures is shown across the bottom of the chart.*

ature to expect. You can then dress as if you were going to be outside in those tem-peratures.

Several other factors should be considered when using the chart. Relative humidity will affect the relative riding temperature appreciably. When humidity is high, the riding temperature will be lower than when it's dry, because as your clothing gets damp or even wet (as in fog), its insulating properties are reduced. Also, some fairings offer better protection than others. Riders with minimal wind protection must com-pensate for this by dressing more warmly. And some people simply get colder than others; generally, you will be aware of this and will know to dress for the colder side of the projected temperature range.

Staying cool is another matter—one that can only be slightly affected by how we dress. I have a self-imposed rule about never riding without helmet, gloves, leather jacket, long pants and boots, so that doesn't leave much room for flexibility. This self-imposed rule came through a great deal of practical experience—a rider's most invaluable tool—and some of it has been less than pleasant. But even if you adopt the same rule, there are still a few options for beating the heat. The simplest one is *when* to ride. In really hot weather, I roll with the first light. I prefer early stops anyway, but it's almost imperative when temperatures hit the 100-degree mark before noon. This is also the most pleasant time of day. Traffic is reasonably light, so riding is more enjoyable. If I start early it also means I can stop early, at an air-conditioned motel or campsite (preferably near water) to cool down before the crowds arrive.

If I'm forced to ride through the desert during the hot part of the day, I add clothes rather than delete them. A heavy cotton, long-sleeved shirt, soaked with water, is worn under a leather jacket which offers controlled evaporation and keeps me surprisingly comfortable. Wetting down jeans works, but not as well, because the water tends to evaporate more rapidly.

On occasion, I have used a riding suit as an outer layer for desert riding in summer, soaking everything underneath. A light-colored or silver suit is best because it reflects heat, while heavy quilted linings are the least desirable because they take so long to dry out. Suits with full-length leg zippers and a double-pull zipper on the front allow a more controlled evaporation, the only drawback being wrinkled clothing. This practice of clothes-wetting only works in areas of low humidity, like the deserts of the Southwest. The best bet (but admittedly not always practicable) is to get an early start and spend the hottest part of the day lounging beside a swimming pool sipping a cool drink.

Now we come down to what I would call the basis of my entire dressing philosophy, upon which I have only touched so far. The concept is not new, but its applicability to motorcycle touring is unquestionable. The key to the idea of *layering* is versatility—a rider's best friend. Layering allows for small adjustments in order to achieve fairly precise temperature control, and it is easier to pack a number of smaller, lighter garments than one large, bulky item. Using this philosophy, it is easy to see the advantages of, for example, taking a light jacket and a down vest to do double duty, instead of a light jacket for warm weather and a heavy one that may only be utilized in extreme cold, if at all. The down vest packs with less bulk and is more versatile, as it can be worn in a variety of situations.

Possibly the only disadvantage of layering is a somewhat bulky look at times, especially for the coldest temperatures. Layering also requires a fair number of garments to be carried along, but they will all function in combination, so when it's the coldest, the touring rider will wear everything. But this allows single garments to be removed as the temperature warms. Another desirable feature is the ability to select a riding wardrobe so that changes for temperature control don't require privacy. Changes can be made along the road in full view of passing motorists without embarrassment to you or to them. This also simplifies meal or rest stops. You can suit up or pull off layers right in front of a restaurant in plain view without feeling uncomfortable.

While comfort, safety and protection are major considerations in dressing properly, they aren't the only ones. Two kinds of comfort are associated with one's clothes—physical and emotional comfort—emotional comfort meaning how you feel about how

Dressing for safety doesn't mean being uncomfortable or looking "odd." Boots, jeans and a shirt are quickly converted to safe mild-weather riding gear by the addition of jacket, helmet and gloves.

you look and what you feel others think of you. While this won't matter much to some people, others will find it a major consideration. But most riders will fall somewhere in between; it matters, but not a great deal. This gets all wrapped up with self-image and what you want to project about yourself (real or fancied) by your dress.

The section that follows will help you implement your clothing choices by presenting the individual components of any good clothing system. It will require some trial and error on your part to determine which clothing combinations work the best under various conditions and which provide you with the greatest sense of physical comfort, protection and personal expression. But if you are conscious about what you take (and don't take), your clothing will be equal to any occasion—from mosquito protection at a swampy campsite to dining at a first-class supper club.

A Clothing System

A clothing "system" is intended to provide both a starting point for new riders and some possible alternatives for the experienced ones. This clothing system is one that I feel quite strongly about. I have constantly refined it over the years. This is not to say it will never change, but it does work. I have tested it over many hundreds of thousands of miles, so I know it works. Being analytical by nature, and having had the chance through my work with *Rider* magazine to test everything on the market, I can assure you that nothing about selection of this system is frivolous.

Undershorts. The first requirement is comfort—each rider should select the style and material that is most comfortable, mainly because undershorts cover one of the major sources of discomfort when touring, that area of the body that comes in contact with the motorcycle seat. For longer trips, especially if riding two-up, there is one other consideration—packing bulk. This is where the ladies have an advantage, as they have traditionally used nylon undergarments, which not only pack small, but dry quickly. This means you will be able to rinse out a pair of nylon briefs and dry them overnight, allowing you to pack fewer garments. Nylon briefs are also advantageous if they get soaked in the rain as they dry quickly. Nylon briefs for men are now on the market and are frequently labeled "European Style."

Undershirt. This is where the actual layering begins, because the undershirt or T-shirt is not just an undergarment but an outer one, as well. For this reason, I select colored fashions with pockets, as I feel more comfortable with this style as an outer garment, either on or off the motorcycle, and it is lightweight enough to be worn under other clothes. The best material is 100% cotton, because it absorbs perspiration in hot weather without becoming clammy or uncomfortable, and it offers quite a bit of warmth under a long-sleeved shirt in cooler weather.

Socks. For all-around wearability, white athletic socks, made with a high percentage of cotton, are hard to beat. In really cold weather, I substitute one or two pairs of medium-weight wool socks for cotton, if they don't hamper the fit of my boots, because tight boots are a direct cause of cold feet and will totally defeat the purpose of warmer socks. Wool also retains its insulation capabilities when wet, which makes it a good foul-weather sock material.

Thermal Underwear. Thermal underwear, or "long johns," offer quite a bit of warmth for their bulk, but they have several drawbacks for touring riders. Thermal underwear usually consists of a long-sleeved top and elastic-waisted bottoms with narrow cuffs that make them difficult, if not impossible, to remove with boots on. The layering system is defeated because use of the bottoms requires nearly total undressing in private, limiting their versatility and confining their use to extremely cold weather where it is reasonable to assume you will be wearing them all day. In actual practice, I reserve long johns for "off-season" tours—in the early spring and late fall or winter— and even then I only utilize the bottom half. Long-john tops lack versatility, as they can usually only be worn under other garments, while a sweater of equal warmth can be worn under a shirt or worn as an outer garment off the bike. I have found the Damart double-force models to be the warmest for their bulk; they are relatively expensive, but do an excellent job. The least expensive, and quite serviceable, are the cotton "waffle weave" models available almost everywhere. The style I have been using the past few seasons is silk long-john bottoms. Currently, the only source I know of for these is the Orvis catalog (for the address of both Damart and Orvis, see the section on catalog sales). Most long johns, worn under an electrically-heated garment, tend to reduce the amount of heat reaching the body, but not the silk style. The silk long-john bottoms are very versatile and add a surprising amount of warmth, yet are comfortable under a pair of jeans up to around 75 degrees F. off the bike. They add virtually no bulk when worn or packed, and they seem to breathe very well, so walking or hiking in them is entirely practical. Like the Damart thermals, silk long johns are expensive, but worth it. They can be rinsed out and squeezed partially dry in a towel and will completely dry overnight.

Pants. Just about any pants can be worn when riding, but it's hard to beat the ubiquitous jeans for practicality. They are sturdy, inexpensive, don't show dirt or soil readily and offer fair abrasion protection. They can be worn as an outer garment on or off the bike, or worn under other layers for cold weather riding. (See *Chaps/Leather Pants.*)

Shirts. As with pants, a wide variety of shirts are suitable for riding, but some are better suited than others. One style that combines all the desirable qualities—versatility, looks, comfort—is the western-style shirt. It comes in an infinite variety of colors and patterns, but the best for riding have long sleeves with snap-close cuffs at the wrists. Size-wise, it is best to pick a sleeve length a couple of inches longer than you would normally wear, so the sleeves won't pull up when you are in riding position. You will want a tight wrist, though, so the sleeves don't hang down to your knuckles when you get off the bike. The best brands or styles are the ones with an extra snap at the cuff to close off that opening (a feature you'll appreciate in mosquito country). Most western shirts have a pair of handy breast pockets with flaps and snap closures. In addition, the western shirt is usually styled rather slim, but with generous shirttails that stay tucked in when you assume your riding position. These shirts come in cotton and wool, from very lightweight to very heavy. For most summer touring, I take along one made of the lightest cotton and one of medium-weight cotton. If I plan to ride in the mountains or expect cooler weather, I will add a third shirt made of either heavy cotton (called chamois cloth) or wool. This not only gives me a change when one shirt gets dirty, but allows a selection of weights to match prevailing temperatures. I always select the long-sleeved styles because, as my Uncle George once pointed out, "You can always roll up long sleeves, but I've never figured out how to roll down short ones."

Boots. Basically, a riding boot can be any pair of sturdy boots, preferably leather, that offer good ankle protection. I prefer those that are at least 12 to 14 inches high for added shin protection against flying debris. The most critical area is the sole of the boot, which should *not* be leather, mainly because the slick leather sole is not conducive to solid footing while straddling a heavy bike. When stopped at a stoplight, some traction is required in order to keep your feet on the ground—and leather doesn't do this, either. Smooth gum soles are only slightly better. A good neoprene or waffle stomper sole is best. Just about any style will do—lace-up, zipper, or pull-on are fine. I like the western-style cowpoke boots for all-around use, but I wear a lace-up style when doing a lot of camping and/or hiking. The higher and heavier models are preferable for cold weather touring.

Sweaters. I like the versatility of sweaters, as well as the way they feel and fit. The turtleneck style is very practical for riding because a rider's neck seems to be an especially vulnerable place for cold breezes. For really cold weather tours, I frequently wear a pullover sweater of medium weight that features a neck that is zipped down to form a collar. I wear this over a T-shirt and under a regular shirt. This way I can pull off the shirt and unzip the sweater for quite a bit of temperature control. My favorite style is the medium-weight, zip-front cardigan sweater that also features zippered turtleneck styling. This sweater has outstanding versatility, as it can be slipped on over a T-shirt or shirt and worn under a leather jacket for quite a bit of warmth without an excess of bulk. The zippered turtleneck offers good temperature control while riding, yet the sweater can be dressy enough to wear off the bike. It could even be used as a substitute for a sports jacket with shirt and tie. Obviously, many styles of sweaters are viable for touring use, but I would avoid the heavy, bulky styles that take extra space to pack and end up being too bulky under other clothing. An excellent alternative to a sweater is one of the jogging or warm-up suit tops. Most feature the zippered turtleneck style that offers good temperature control. They are certainly acceptable for wear off the bike as a light jacket and can be also worn under a leather jacket without too much bulk. Granted, they aren't as dressy as a cardigan sweater, but for the jogger who plans to run while on tour, it is a great dual-purpose item. I would even go so far as to recommend using the jogging pants instead of long johns for wear under regular pants when it's cold, as their dual use for jogging goes along with the premise of making each garment serve as many purposes as possible.

Vests. I am personally addicted to vests, whether they are made of nylon and down, leather or denim, with or without electric heat. I have found vests to be extremely versatile and perfect for riding. They pack small, yet offer a great deal of warmth for their weight and bulk, mainly because they put their insulation where it will do the most good—directly over the "core" of the body. Strange as it may seem, if my hands get cold while riding, all I have to do is put on a vest and warmer gloves will not usually be necessary. This is because blood circulation to extremities, the hands and feet, is reduced when the body's core temperature begins to drop. Regardless of style or material, the vest you select should offer a fairly trim fit. When used for warmth it will be worn under other garments, especially a leather jacket, and for the coldest temperatures it will be combined with a sweater, shirt and T-shirt. For this reason I would not select the bulkier down vests on the market, as they are more difficult to pack and too bulky for wear under a regular jacket. As for which style to choose, it mainly depends on your style of touring. If you are planning to go camping, fishing or hiking, I would select an all-nylon down vest. It packs very small, is extremely versatile on or off the bike and offers an "outdoorsy" look. For pure riding versatility and temperature control, I find the electric vests the best choice, especially those that are thermostatically controlled. However, while they offer some warmth off the bike (with no electrical connection), they are not nearly as good in that respect as the down models. For pure good looks, nothing matches a finely tailored leather vest. The leather offers versatility and warmth, but won't cause you to be excluded from some of the nicer eating establishments because you are improperly dressed.

Jacket. Wearing a leather jacket isn't mandatory, but it offers so many benefits and is so superior to anything else available that it is hardly worth considering the alternatives. Probably the only drawback of leather is cost; but when you consider the years of wear a good leather jacket will give you, it is a bargain-basement buy. Because leather breathes, it is not the warmest garment available, but this same feature makes it extremely versatile for controlling temperature. I wear a leather jacket all the time on a bike. The best jackets are lined with a single layer of nylon material or very light padding. If you think of a leather jacket as basic body protection for riding—like your helmet and gloves—everything else starts to fall in place. In accordance with the layering system, you can add or remove layers over or under the jacket for temperature control, but the jacket is always worn when on the bike. As an outer riding garment, a leather jacket offers many benefits besides abrasion protection. It offers protection against flying objects (bugs, etc.), doesn't flap in the wind and can be found with a variety of features designed expressly for motorcycle riding, including zippered cuffs to keep wind and critters from blowing up your sleeves. A good jacket will feature wind flaps behind or over front zippers, and most contain snug neck closures. All these features are desirable for riding. By opening the cuffs a little, and drawing down the front zipper with just a T-shirt underneath, a leather jacket is quite comfortable for even hot weather.

Off the bike, a leather jacket is good-looking and can be used for a number of activities. Virtually any style that includes tight closures at the wrists and neck, and is long enough for comfort when seated on the bike, can be considered a suitable riding jacket. An inside pocket is handy, as are one or two outside pockets with positive closures. Zip-out liners are clever, but I find that a vest will serve the same purpose and is more versatile for touring. While there are a number of styles available, my motto is "the plainer the better". As mentioned, a leather jacket should offer adjustable neck and wrist closures for wind protection and some form of adjustment at the waist. Fit is also important. The jacket should provide enough room to wear a shirt, sweater and vest underneath (the best way to tell is to try it on while wearing these garments), but not be uncomfortably big with just a T-shirt underneath. This extra room with just a T-shirt can be desirable, because it means you will get good air circulation for hot weather riding. The sleeves should be long enough to be comfortable in a riding position; check to see that sitting in a riding position doesn't pull the back of the jacket up above the belt.

One word about down jackets. While they are great for off-bike wear, they lack many important features for riding. Namely, they give scant abrasion protection, and when exposed to wind, the down compresses and loses nearly all its insulating qualities, so it lacks warmth when it's needed the most. A down vest/leather jacket combination is a much better choice.

Chaps/Leather Pants. Here is one item of wear that is almost exclusively used when riding. Leather pants or chaps are virtually useless for off-bike wear, but they offer some very important features for riding, not the least of which is abrasion protection. Also, they don't flap in the wind and they offer considerable warmth. One of the biggest drawbacks of leather pants is they can be so damned hot when you are not on the bike. Since it is such a hassle to change pants (removing boots, then switching the belt and contents of the pockets), I used to find myself not wearing them, even when they were packed in my saddlebags. The solution was chaps, worn over jeans. Leather chaps offer nearly all the protection and other good features of leather pants, yet can be unzipped and slipped off when stepping off the bike, just like the leather jacket. Most riders will find chaps comfortable most of the time—even when riding in weather up to around

Chaps offer nearly the same protection as leather pants, but are more versatile.

Black chaps from Harley-Davidson. Custom made chaps, left, by Sharold Leathers.

75 or 80 degrees—because their open design offers better air circulation. Because they are easier to take off and put on, they will be worn more often. For maximum versatility, it would be convenient to have an electrically heated, insulated, removable liner. Important features to look for in chaps are (1) full-length zippers down each leg (the ones on the inside of the leg are easier to operate than those running down the back), (2) a soft and fairly narrow belt that doesn't bind or dig into your midriff area, (3) an adjustable waistband in addition to the belt and (4) flaps tucked under the material at the hip that can be pulled out to form a leather crotch cover for additional warmth and protection. If the color of the chaps is selected to match your riding jacket, it not only looks sharp but makes a complete leather outfit for riding.

Gloves. First and foremost, gloves provide protection from abrasion in case of a spill and from pain and injury from flying objects or cold weather. Gloves also help keep hands from getting stiff and sore from long stints on the bike by providing a cushion between hands and grips. It's hard to think about wearing gloves when riding across the desert in 120-degree weather, but most experienced riders are aware of the trade-offs—hands are susceptible to sunburn and dryness from exposure to heat as well as cold. When riding in warm or hot weather, an unlined deerskin glove is best, offering the thickness needed for protection, yet being breathable enough to be worn in the hottest temperatures.

For summer touring, it is advisable to carry at least two pairs of gloves. The unlined gloves are fine for most daytime touring in good weather, but I always bring along a warmer pair in the event the weather turns cold or wet. The most versatile gloves for this use are the kind that offer a removable nylon rain mitt, which doesn't really keep out the rain, but does add considerable warmth. When touring in mountain country, or early or late in the season, I usually bring along another pair of hand warmers, such as a pair of good heavy mittens. Fit is probably the most important consideration when selecting touring gloves, espcially if you want to keep your hands warm. Tight gloves mean cold hands. A good way to determine fit is to wrap your hands, with the gloves on, around the handlebars of your bike. For proper fit, the tips of your fingers should not press against the ends of the gloves and should provide plenty of room. When buying mittens for cold weather wear, get them large enough to be able to wear a pair of soft cloth gloves underneath. Damart makes a very nice glove for under-mitten-wear that adds a big margin of warmth, but doesn't take up much room in your tank bag.

Cowhide is the most common leather used in gloves and mittens and is fine for all models, although deerskin is preferable for the unlined gloves. Incidentally, while color is a personal choice, in the unlined models you might want to select a color as close to your own skin tone as possible, since the dyes will tend to stain your hands when you perspire. With the heavier gloves and mittens, pay attention to the type of lining used, as it will have a great bearing on how well they insulate. Foam-backed nylon seems to offer the best insulation, while the thick pile lining found in some models is the least desirable, offering not nearly the warmth its bulk would suggest and taking far too long to dry out when wet. An acceptable compromise is a glove with foam lining on the palm side, and fleece lining on the back of the gloves or mittens.

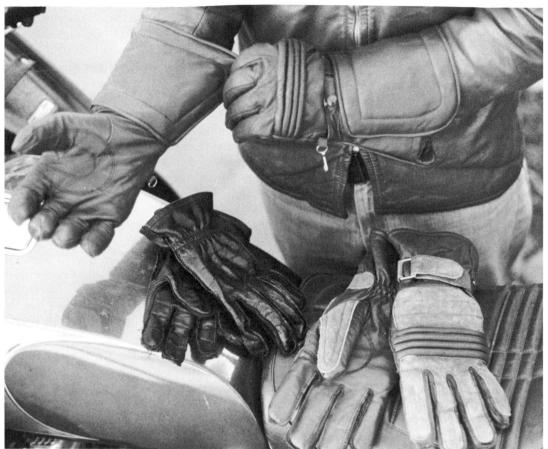

Three pairs of gloves in different weights is not unreasonable for summer touring.

Gauntleted gloves, on rider, are good for temperatures down to around 45 degrees.

Rainwear

The term "waterproof" has, in my opinion, been used far too lightly in regard to clothing. As far as I'm concerned, waterproof should mean that absolutely no water gets inside a suit or garment. But a real working definition of this word should include the conditions under which any item of clothing could be considered truly waterproof. And since we are talking about motorcycling and its inherent exposure to a host of riding conditions, I will attempt to define the terms *waterproof, water repellent* and *water resistant* as they relate to motorcycle riding.

Waterproof—When a rainsuit is worn for 12 hours straight on a motorcycle (with or without a fairing), in various intensities of rain from moderate to heavy downpours, and the clothing worn under the suit is still dry, that's my definition of waterproof.

Water repellent—When the rainwear in question will keep a rider's clothing dry for at least two hours in heavy rain or four hours in light to moderate rain on a moving motorcycle, it can be considered water repellent.

Water resistant—Will keep a rider dry for 30 minutes in light to moderate rain.

Unfortunately, very few items on the market today under the heading of rainwear are truly waterproof according to the above definition. But it is fair to say that any rainsuit is better than none; even a garment that lets in a lot of water will still serve part of its function by keeping out most of the wind and thus preserve some warmth. I consider rainwear an absolute must for touring, regardless of when, where and how long you will be touring. Rain gear packs small, is usable in a variety of circumstances and is almost impossible to get along without in rain or heavy mist. Rainwear holds a position in that special class of items, along with first aid gear, that might not be used on every trip, but still deserves a place in your pack.

The basic item of apparel for rainy weather is a rainsuit, but with the variety of styles and materials on the market, how does one choose? Those good-looking, one-piece suits are still best for long stints in the rain, but they require a bit more work to put on and remove, and are not at all convenient if you just want to pop out for a quick ride to a nearby restaurant in a light rain. Another drawback is the fold that is created in the front of the suit when one is in a seated position. Generally, this fold includes a portion of the front zipper, so if the fold creates a pocket, it will eventually leak water through the zipper. The remedy is simple, however. When you sit down, check this fold and turn it so it doesn't hold water. Another drawback of one-piece suits is lack of versatility. When camping and doing anything strenuous, like hauling wood or setting up a tent, the two-piece suit will allow much better ventilation when the bottom of the jacket is left loose. When riding, the one-piece suits tend to be warmer, a desirable trait in cool weather, but unpleasant when it's hot. One last consideration in the one-piece vs. two-piece design question is pants pocket accessibility. One-piece suits usually limit access more than two-piece designs. Overall, the one-piece suits tend to keep you dryer on the bike, but offer less convenience and versatility.

Rainwear is produced in a variety of materials, all with varying degrees of water repellency. You can find anything from polyurethane film to a fairly heavyweight nylon. I would leave the very lightweight suit made of polyurethane film (usually the least expensive) to the commuting riders, who would probably carry it only as an emergency-type garment. The touring rider will require more utilitarian service from rainwear than these offer. Touring riders can expect to spend days in their rainsuits at times, so it is not an item to skimp on. The weight of the material is a trade-off between light-weight suits that pack well but don't hold up under extended use, and heavier suits that provide long wear but are bulky to pack. And packed is where most rainsuits tend to stay, so this can be an important consideration.

There is one rather special type of rainsuit fabric that deserves mention, because it is considered to be a rather revolutionary step in waterproof materials. Gore-Tex has been designed to shed liquid water (like rain) but allow the escape of water vapor, in the form of moisture generated from the body. The idea is sensational, except for one flaw. The material has proven to be very sensitive to road grime, dirt and oily dirt—

and these tend to destroy the special properties of this wonder cloth. To compound the problem, this material is used in some extremely versatile and functional garments, such as rainsuits and mountaineering parkas that are perfect riding gear. But the constant exposure to dirt, especially to the lower extremities, pretty much rules out the use of Gore-Tex pants for motorcycle use, because after only one or two wearings, these pants leak pretty badly. The parkas are a little less susceptible and offer some marvelous benefits. They are designed for strenuous outdoor activity, like camping and hiking, and are cut quite long with plenty of pockets. The Gore-Tex parkas are very expensive, priced at least as much or more than most top-of-the-line rainsuits, and are usually available with matching pants made of urethane-coated nylon. The parkas make excellent rainwear on the bike, featuring good hoods and wide sleeve openings that will fit over rain mitts. Best of all, the parkas really show their worth when riding in hot, muggy weather, where perspiration can make you as wet as the rain. These Gore-Tex parkas breathe, keeping you dry even in really hot weather. (See the catalog section in Chapter 8 on camping for a listing of Gore-Tex parka suppliers.)

What are the features to look for when selecting rain gear? To begin with, check the seams; they should be welded or sewn. If sewn, there should be a shiny layer of sealant over the seams. Some manufacturers provide a seam sealant with their suits and let the purchaser do the sealing because it is too costly and time-consuming. This practice is acceptable if the suit is of high quality at a reasonable price, because the price would probably be considerably higher if the manufacturer did the sealing. Check seams carefully for gaps or openings in the sealant. One way to do this is to look inside the suit and examine the material and seams, using a bright light outside; any breaks will show up as points of light. If you discover any flaws, either reject the suit or accept the fact that it will leak everywhere there is a point of light.

Closures, especially those at the neck, are a key to keeping out water and should allow enough latitude so they can be closed to any degree of tightness you desire under varying weather conditions. Suitable closures include elastic bands, snaps or Velcro tabs. Fit is another important consideration and the legs on any rainsuit should be large enough to allow you to slip the pants on over boots. I have always made it a point to try to select rainsuits that have sleeves large enough to go over the gauntlets of my gloves, even when I wear rain mitts on the gloves. Unfortunately, this feature is often overlooked by rainsuit manufacturers. When riding in the rain, water tends to run down the back of the arms, which means it will end up inside your gloves if the gauntlet is on the outside of the sleeve. The sleeve, worn over the gauntlet, effectively prevents this and keeps out the wind, as well.

The front zipper is probably the most difficult to seal, but it should feature a generous flap that fastens down with snaps or Velcro strips. Two-piece suits should offer good overlap at the waist of the pants and a jacket that is at least 12 inches below the waist when standing; otherwise it will create a gap when you are seated on the bike. The jacket should offer some way to draw in the bottom to keep it from flapping and to prevent water from seeping in underneath. On the subject of hoods, I find them to be an asset in heavy rains. A lightweight hood can be worn under the helmet and

will all but eliminate water running down the back. As many hoods can be uncomfortably hot in warm weather, the best type for year-round use is one that tucks under
the collar until needed. Bright yellow or orange are the most popular colors in rain
gear as they offer a degree of visibility for auto drivers when it's needed the most—
under the adverse conditions of rain.

Some suits are sold as kits and are worth spending a few extra dollars on. Usually,
these kits include boot and hand covers. If you don't select a suit that comes with these,
both are available separately. Lightweight rain mitts are certainly worthwhile. They
will not only keep your gloves dry, but do contribute to hand warmth, whether it's
raining or not. Rain mitts are available at motorcycle shops, but can also be found at
most sporting goods stores as snow mitt covers. Most models will need to have the
seams sealed with a good sealant for motorcycle use in rain, but this is a minor chore.
For keeping feet as dry as possible, I find rubber boots are best. Lightweight "Totes"
are fine; they pack small and are relatively inexpensive, but tend to be quite narrow.
They are also extremely difficult to locate. I purchased mine years ago at L.L. Beans
in Maine, but they had stopped handling them the last time I checked. A good alternative
is to purchase zippered dress overshoes; they are bulkier to pack, but hold up quite
well if you can find a pair that fit over your regular riding boots.

For face protection in the rain, I find the full-coverage helmet superior to anything
else I have tried. It allows less water to swirl up around the face which will improve
visibility immensely. This is a special concern for riders who wear glasses.

Riding Suits

Many riders consider a riding suit the only weather protection necessary, so why
not just select a good riding suit and forget about layering? My contention is that
versatility and temperature control are the keys to personal comfort, which riding suits
sadly lack as a sole riding garment. Riding suits are a relatively recent development,
at least the modern suits that are currently available. The waxed cotton suits from
England have been around for many years and in some respects are the forerunners
of today's riding suits. Incidentally, these waxed cotton suits are still available and
some very experienced riders still swear by them. They are waterproof, if the wax
coating is kept in good condition, and do offer some warmth. Their main value is that
they offer a totally windproof outer layer with good neck, wrist and ankle seals, plus
a fabric with good body. However, there are some serious drawbacks. The waxed finish
is black and rubs off on *everything*—the bike seat, the rider's clothing and anything it
comes in contact with in the pack. These suits can be quite stiff in cold weather and
become soft and clammy in hot weather. But the concept of a medium-weight, windproof and waterproof riding suit is an excellent way to go. Many of the riding suits on
the market today owe more design allegiance to the snowmobile suit than these English
riding suits, however. In general, these riding outfits feature fairly bulky insulation
which is an attraction, because they are quite warm, but it is also a detraction, in that
they offer limited versatility for the touring rider. These suits also don't offer the temperature latitude that is so desirable for the rider who will be spending some long

hours on the bike. This is especially true of the heavier, winter-weight suits, with six or seven ounces of insulation per yard. But weight is only one consideration.

If you look at a riding suit as only one part of your clothing system, it is easier to select the style that will offer the maximum benefits. Nearly all the newer suits on the market use urethane-backed nylon as an outer layer, which turns out to be the best choice. Trailex, a fabric blended of Antron nylon and rayon, offers some benefits, but has one serious drawback. In general, riding suits are not billed as waterproof, and some don't even qualify as water repellent, usually because no attempt has been made to seal the seams. With urethane-backed nylon, the material itself is waterproof, but the seams will admit water. In the case of Trailex, the fabric tends to stretch with continued use and wear—becoming less water-resistant as time goes on. The Trailex does offer greater abrasion resistance than plain nylon, but the loss of water and wind resistance through wear considerably reduces its usefulness for motorcycle touring. The urethane-backed nylon commonly used is susceptible to heat damage, including contact with a hot exhaust pipe or friction from abrasion. Otherwise, this material holds up well and stays wind resistant and watertight through continued use. It is also relatively lightweight, which helps reduce packing bulk. Most rainsuits offer polyester insulation, quilted to the lining, which works well as this synthetic material doesn't compress and lose its insulation properties from wind pressure. Conversely, it makes the suits bulkier to pack. Lining materials are usually a nylon/taffeta blend which is smooth and wears well and contributes greatly to ease in donning and doffing the suit over clothing and boots. Full-length leg zippers are another desirable feature that allow quick and easy on-or-off operation; these zippers should have double pulls so they will allow access to a pants pocket under the suit. The zippers also offer a form of temperature control, allowing for a little extra ventilation without removing the suit.

As with rainsuits, closures are especially important. The neck closure should fit snugly and be made of a non-irritating material. Padded nylon works quite well, but corduroy does nearly as well on the inside of a traditional mandarin-type collar found on nearly all riding suits. The closures should offer some degree of adjustability for size, so the suit can be worn as tightly as desired for water protection and temperature control. Velcro tabs work well, and knitted wrist cuffs on the inside of the sleeves are common, but there should also be an outer closure to cut off drafts that can penetrate even knitted cuffs; gauntleted gloves or mittens can also cut down on drafts. Ankle closure isn't quite as critical, but there should be some means of reducing the size of the leg opening to keep drafts from going up the legs when maximum warmth is desired. Windproofing is an important benefit of these suits, so any breach caused by poor closures will reduce their effectiveness as riding garments.

In addition to neck, wrist and ankle closures, there is the big zipper down the front to consider. If left exposed to the wind, it will be a major source of drafts. Therefore, all quality suits will feature a wind flap over or under this zipper. Check to see that the flap has separate fasteners, such as Velcro strips or snaps, if it is incorporated on the outside of the suit. Leg zippers aren't as critical, but they should have some form of wind flap over or under them for the same reasons. Riding suits, like rainsuits, are available in one- or two-piece models, with the major difference being price. The one-piece models are considerably less expensive and eliminate most drafts between jacket and pants. But it is possible to purchase a two-piece suit that has pants that come up as high as your shirt pockets, which not only eliminates cold air but puts a double layer of insulation over the critical core area of the body. The big advantage of the two-piece style is versatility. The jacket can be worn alone on shorter trips and doesn't require a major effort to put on or remove. A jacket of this sort, while less versatile than a leather jacket, is a viable option.

Unless you are planning extensive cold-weather riding, or use a riding suit only for commuting purposes, I would forego the heavier and warmer suits for a lighter-weight suit with two to four ounces of insulation. Ideally, this type of riding suit will fit comfortably over a leather jacket and chaps, but will prove trim enough to wear under a rainsuit. The English-made suits tend to be the most water-repellent, perhaps because of the high percentage of inclement days in the British Isles. Most really water-repellent suits won't feature full-length leg zippers, but if the pants are easy to pull on and off over riding boots, this is not a design flaw. Outside pockets on a riding suit are handy, but pretty much a personal choice.

When selecting a riding suit, check all closures as well as quality of construction. Are the seams straight and continuous? Are they double or triple stitched? Are there extra stitches at stress points, like under the arms and in the crotch? In general, if all visible parts show careful construction, the rest of the suit will be made the same way.

Fit of a riding suit is very important; be sure to try it on over all the clothes you will be wearing for coldest conditions and ensure there are no really tight spots, especially when sitting. To check for fit, either sit on a bike in a riding position or, if that's not possible, sit on a straight-backed chair backwards, with the back between your legs and stretch your arms forward. This should point out any shortness in the legs or arms. It's much better for arms and legs of riding apparel to be a little too long than too short.

Electrical Clothing

During World War II, electrical clothing was developed for bomber crews, and it worked for them just as the modern adaptation of that clothing works for the motorcycle rider. Full riding suits are available with built-in electrical heating as well as separate vests and leg covers, electric gloves and socks. Do-it-yourself wiring kits can be installed in garments you already own.

All of this clothing works on a simple principle. Electrical current from the bike's 12-volt system is channeled through wires that have mild electrical resistance and they heat up when current is applied. It works essentially the same as an electric blanket, but the 12-volt DC current used for riding clothes is much safer than the 115-volt AC current used for electric blankets. It's impossible to receive any kind of a shock from the 12-volt clothing, even if it's soaking wet.

While the full riding suit with electric heating is very warm, it suffers the same lack of versatility as the big snowmobile-type winter riding suits. The electric vest, and to a lesser degree the matching electric chaps or leg covers, offers a great deal of versatility in the form of temperature control while riding. When these garments are combined with a thermostat, they allow considerable adjustment of heat. While electrical clothing doesn't eliminate the other garments in the system, it complements them greatly.

Shown above is a Widder electric vest with a thermostat for temperature control. The styling is simple, but functional. Electrically heated garments are becoming increasingly popular, and have special appeal for the touring motorcyclist.

Back to Basics

So far we have treated each garment separately, but we call the combination of garments a "system," suggesting they will work best in different combinations. That's exactly the case. Let's outline a specific hypothetical clothing system for a touring rider. For this discussion, cost isn't the major factor. It must be considered, but function has a higher priority.

Our hypothetical rider is setting out on a summer tour, starting fairly late in the morning, say around 9 or 10 a.m. His tour will include riding at fairly high elevations in the Western states. He anticipates getting into cool temperatures.

Since he starts late, we can dress our hypothetical rider for fairly hot weather (above 75 degrees F.) in light cotton briefs, cotton T-shirt (crew-neck style, with a single breast pocket), jeans, cotton/nylon blend athletic-style socks, and neoprene-soled, pull-on riding boots. Before getting on the bike, he dons a leather jacket, full-coverage helmet and unlined deerskin riding gloves. In his touring gear loaded on the bike is a cotton western-style shirt with long sleeves and a cardigan-style, medium-weight sweater that zips up to form a turtleneck collar. An electric vest and matching electric chaps are rolled up and tucked in the side pocket of his frame-mounted fairing, along with the thermostat for the electric garments. The bike is already wired with electrical connections for the clothing. A pair of leather chaps is tucked away, in addition to a good quality, two-piece rainsuit plus waterproof mitts and a pair of rubber boots. In the fairing are a pair of medium-weight riding gloves with nylon-faced foam linings.

As our rider travels, the temperature climbs to around the 90-degree mark, but although he is warm, his perspiration under the jacket (which is now open at the lower arms and partly unzipped in front) evaporates and the jacket does a good job of keeping him comfortable. As the sun drops, the temperature does, as well—so at the next gas stop he adds the long-sleeved western shirt, changes to the heavier gloves and zips on the chaps for the last leg of the day. The temperature at this point is only down around 75 degrees, but he knows he is headed into higher elevations and the sun has now set. As a last-minute decision he adds the electric vest over the shirt and under the jacket. He doesn't turn it on and doesn't even have to fully zip up the jacket—yet. As the temperature drops below 60 degrees, he zips up the jacket and is glad he added the chaps. As he nears his destination for the night, he has climbed in elevation and the temperature is still dropping. It's now in the low 50s so he turns on the electric vest and reaches his destination an hour or so later, tired but warm, comfortable and still alert.

Starting out the next morning the thermometer is down around 40 degrees (a little cool for this time of year, due to the higher elevation), so he selects the same outfit used during the previous day, except he adds electric chaps under his leather chaps and adds the cardigan-style sweater under the jacket, over the electric vest, long-sleeved shirt and T-shirt. He uses the rain mitts over his gloves since he didn't bring any mittens. While he is comfortable at these temperatures, if it had been much below 35 degrees, he would have added the rainsuit over everything and would still have been comfortable. At that temperature our rider would have been approaching the lower limit of the system he carried.

As the day warms up to around 50 degrees, he first removes the rain mitts, electric chaps and sweater. Now he is in the same outfit used at the end of the previous day. Actually, he could substitute the sweater for the electric vest, but it wouldn't offer quite the variability of the electric garment. When the electric heat is turned off, the sweater would offer slightly more warmth than the vest. But when the vest is turned on, it's much warmer than the sweater. Thus the vest has appreciably greater adjustability.

From this example we can see how the different garments work either separately or together to provide temperature control for real comfort. It's easy to overlook the rainsuit as a garment offering warmth, mainly because it seems too light and flimsy to offer much warmth. But by completely blocking out the wind, and with varying degrees of insulation provided by the other garments, it will add greatly to warmth whether it's raining or not. When the rider is dressed in the lightest outfit (T-shirt, socks, boots, jeans, jacket, helmet and gloves), the rest of the system can easily be carried in a small day pack, yet he is equipped for temperatures down to around freezing or slightly below—more than adequate for nearly all summer touring. Another advantage of this system is that nearly all the garments, with the exception of the electric and leather chaps, are quite usable for off-the-bike wear.

Our rider could substitute a down or leather vest for the electric vest and still be equipped for temperatures down to around 40 or 45 degrees, depending on his personal tolerance level for cold. If the same temperature protection were desired without electric clothing, a medium-weight riding suit could be added. If it is acceptably water repellent, the rainsuit could be deleted. But without first-hand experience with the riding suit, to confirm its water repellency, I wouldn't advise it.

This calls to mind a trick I have found valuable for really bad weather, when one must spend long hours in the rain. It helps to wear a double layer of water repellent clothing—a rainsuit over a riding suit. A second layer of leather works nearly as well. While leather isn't water repellent, it doesn't soak up water as readily as most clothing will. Leathers worn under a rainsuit will repel most or all the small amount of water that gets past the outer layer.

If our hypothetical rider were planning a late fall, winter or early spring tour, a medium-weight riding suit could be added to the previous system (including the electric items), plus a heavier western shirt and a pair of mittens. He probably would include a couple of special purpose items for colder weather, like a silk face mask for under the helmet and possibly would substitute a pair of pile-lined, zippered overshoes for his rubber rain boots. With those changes, he would be equipped to ride comfortably in temperatures down to zero—not the best weather for motorcycling, but if the roads are free of ice, it can be quite pleasant when dressed properly.

While this cold-weather outfit is a little bulkier, with the addition of the mittens, heavier overshoes and riding suit, it's still reasonable in bulk for packing and, of course, our rider is still equipped for any degree of warmer weather that may be encountered,

75° and Over

35-5°

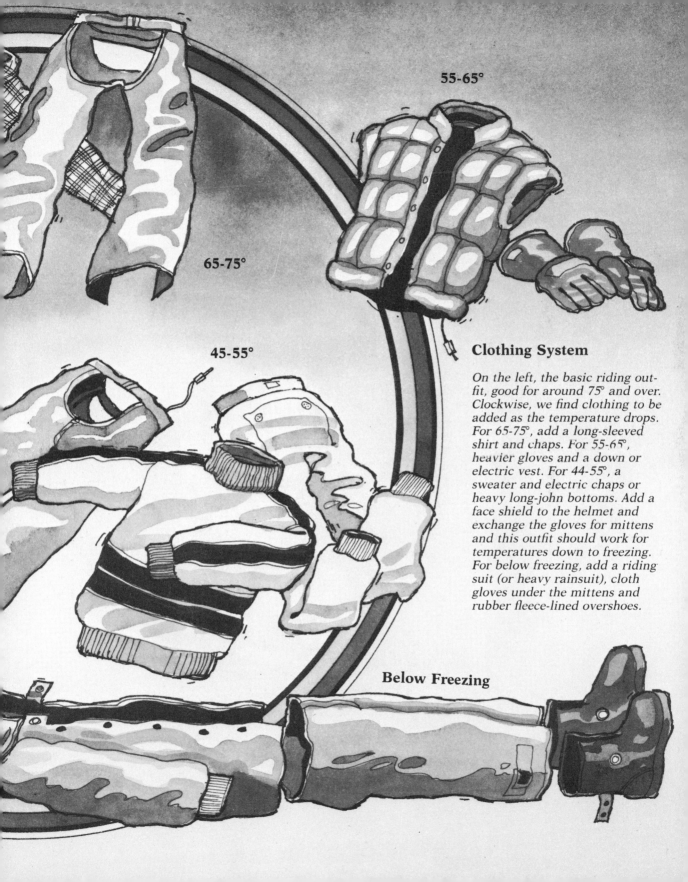

55-65°

65-75°

45-55°

Clothing System

On the left, the basic riding outfit, good for around 75° and over. Clockwise, we find clothing to be added as the temperature drops. For 65-75°, add a long-sleeved shirt and chaps. For 55-65°, heavier gloves and a down or electric vest. For 44-55°, a sweater and electric chaps or heavy long-john bottoms. Add a face shield to the helmet and exchange the gloves for mittens and this outfit should work for temperatures down to freezing. For below freezing, add a riding suit (or heavy rainsuit), cloth gloves under the mittens and rubber fleece-lined overshoes.

Below Freezing

Below 25°, it's pretty much a matter of getting all the clothing on to stay warm. Here we've added a silk face mask and heavy riding suit.

such as the temperature range during a trip from Chicago to Florida and back in mid-February or March.

Actual costs for a system like this will vary, but for planning purposes we can give some price ranges that can be expected. Boots: $50 to $150; leather jacket: $70 to $200; leather chaps: $40 to $125; vest: $35 to $100; leather pants: $60 to $150; helmet: $50 to $150; rainsuit: $40 to $150; riding suit: $100 to $300. Most of the other items listed should not run over $50 each. To calculate the approximate weight of riding clothes, I normally add 15 pounds to each person's weight for helmet, jacket, boots and gloves. For summer touring, I add another 12 pounds; for winter trips, I add 20 pounds extra for additional riding clothes.

Finding the needed garments may prove difficult, especially for those who live outside major metropolitan areas. The best source of clothing, more often than not, is the local motorcycle dealer, which is another good reason to select a dealer who specializes in touring. Some garments can be purchased direct from the manufacturer, but in most cases the dealer is the only one who can order them direct or through a distributor. A number of mail order houses sell riding clothes. Most offer catalog listings. Check for their advertisements in motorcycle magazines. Generally, these mail order firms offer good prices for name-brand products. If finances are a real problem, and everything can't be purchased at one time, simply apply the principles of an outer windproof layer with an insulation layer under it and use whatever other clothing is appropriate for the temperatures you'll be encountering. Probably the best choice for a windproof outer layer is a good rainsuit. It will offer the most versatility for the money. Most wardrobes include some type of boots, jeans, sweaters or sweatshirts and jackets. Adding the rainsuit to these items will create a beginning outfit. Then, as finances permit, the various articles of clothing mentioned here can be added, one at a time.

I have begun to discover that a big part of dealing with adverse weather is dependent upon one's mental attitude. I once saw a photograph of a woman and a child walking together in the rain. While the woman was getting most of the benefit of the umbrella she was carrying, she still appeared to be hating the walk. The child, on the other hand, was enjoying the experience by taking in as much of his surroundings as possible. This kind of attitude, of embracing every turn of the weather with preparedness and good humor, is probably what lies at the bottom of every touring rider's real reason for riding—to challenge the unexpected.

Chapter 6
For Women Riders

For this chapter on women riders, I enlisted the help of Annie Briggs, a British motorcycling journalist who was introduced to motorcycle touring as a passenger. She toured on her own as a fairly inexperienced rider, falling into many of the traps outlined elsewhere in this book.

In this chapter, Annie describes some of the problems and pleasures of being a female touring rider. Many of her experiences will be of interest to both male and female touring motorcyclists . . .

Any woman who decides to go motorcycle touring on her own may as well accept the fact that she will have to explain why she has been driven to this extraordinary behavior. The truth is, whereas it's perfectly acceptable, even admirable, for a man and his motorcycle to tackle the elements, it is generally considered to be quite out of the question for a woman to want to do the same thing.

Perhaps women are moving just a little too fast in the motorcycling world. After all, hardly any time has passed since women left their "rightful" place on the pillion seat and started taking the controls. Now they want to head off into the wilds with only a dumb motorcycle to protect them—and why not? Solo touring can result in some exciting and rewarding experiences, and there is no reason why anyone who wants to go-it-alone should not feel able to do so.

Having said that, touring alone is certainly not for everyone; there are no prizes for suffering a solo trip just to prove you can do it. Any woman with an overactive imagination who sees every strange man as a potential attacker and every unfamiliar environment as a threat to her well-being may as well accept that she is not cut out for solo adventures and should find traveling companions. There's no shame in that. In fact, a lot can be said for touring in groups and for passengering, but we'll get on to that a bit later.

I was a relatively inexperienced rider when I first went motorcycle touring on my own. My initiation into the sport was more circumstance than choice but, as it turned out, it suited me fine.

My bike was a 185cc Suzuki and the journey was a round trip from Britain to West

Berlin. The little Suzuki wasn't the perfect long-distance tourer, but it did its best and I wasn't dissatisfied. However, the motorcycle was badly overloaded, and while traveling along an exposed stretch of autobahn not far from the Dutch border, a sudden gust of strong wind blew us into a roadside ditch. Badly shaken, but otherwise in one piece, I managed to continue on to catch the ferry home and arrived back safely without further incident; a bent swing arm was the only lasting indication that the bike had been touring. That trip taught me quite a lot about solo motorcycle touring, especially from the woman's point of view. I had met and made friends with a great many riders whom I suspect would not have made the effort to stop and befriend me had I been part of a group. Also, I felt better able to deal with my critics who felt it was extremely foolhardy for a teenage girl to go motorcycle touring on her own.

I realized I'd made some pretty fundamental mistakes. I'd taken no spares for the bike and, as the model bike I rode did not exist in West Berlin at that time, it was fortunate that the only spare part I needed was a side panel which fell victim to a souvenir hunter, and that I could manage without. In this case, ignorance really was bliss, but I was left with no doubt about how lucky I'd been. I was constantly stopped by Berliners—riders and non-riders—who asked "How many times did you break down on your way here?" and "Didn't the engine seize under such stress?" That sort of pessimism would be enough to keep you at home, but it does point up the need to live within the machine's capabilities. Now, with many more miles of motorcycle touring behind me, I am at least more aware of my mistakes; I still tend to overload a bike, but that is more through bad habit than lack of knowledge and, after all, one of the big advantages of going solo is that you can take almost everything you need and no one's going to tell you otherwise! (See Chapters 7 and 9 for the right way to do it!)

The biggest single objection you will hear about going off on your own is almost certain to be concern for your safety. Traditionally, women are considered less able to look after themselves than men and, of course, they are often at a physical disadvantage in the event of an attack. However, there is no reason to feel any more vulnerable with a motorcycle than without it; in fact, it seems as if the reverse could even be true. Men often seem to be slightly intimidated by the sight of a woman on a motorcycle, reading it as a clear indication that she is well able to take care of herself. There may be one or two individuals who will see you as an easy pick-up, but on the whole you are likely to be less bothered by unwanted advances while motorcycle touring than while traveling on public transport. It also makes sense to carry some sort of legitimate weapon for use in self-defense, but only if you are really sure you'll use it. Otherwise you run the risk of having it used against you. For over a year now I have carried a spray containing an irritant dye which I would not hesitate to use if I really felt threatened with attack by a human or a wild animal. The dye manufacturer claims the spray will incapacitate an assailant while doing no permanent damage. It is reassuring to have it along.

There are undoubtedly some very real advantages to being a lone female rider. However much you like to believe in equal opportunity, you can be assured of receiving more help en route than any of your male counterparts. Until it's conclusively proven

Passenger comfort and safety should
always be considered. Remember that
the passenger may have an exaggerated
impression of the angle of the bike
around curves, and the heightened
sensation of speed on a motorcycle can
be terrifying to the novice passenger.

that the aid you receive is solely because you are female, surely it is not worth turning down!

So, now you've finally decided to go touring on your own. You've convinced your boyfriend or husband not to take it personally, it's just something you need to do; you've promised to call home every other day just to say you're OK; you've tucked away all those phone numbers and addresses of your mom's and dad's friends, your friends' friends and anyone else you might need to call in an emergency. Now what? Well, the next decision is yours, and the next one, and the next. Making decisions can be one of the hardest things to get used to if you are normally with someone else who makes the decisions most of the time. Suddenly you have days on end of making up your own mind and no one around to change it for you. At times it's great. You feel really independent, your own boss at last, completely in charge and totally self-suffi-cient. Then there are the bad moments—when you are tired and need someone to tell you it's time to stop, that there's no use in pressing on—when the going gets tough and there's no one to share the load.

Loneliness is unavoidable if you travel any distance on your own. There are those moments of beauty that lack something when they cannot be shared; those long, empty roads which suddenly make you feel terribly lost, miles from anything and anyone you know; the lunch stops and motel stops when you feel like chatting over the day's ride and there's no one you feel able to talk to. Any small problem threatens to become a major catastrophe. Your drive chain is looking dry and you've lost your can of lubricant; suddenly your chain looks like it will snap and tangle itself in the engine. That minor spill you took earlier in the day while negotiating a difficult trail out of the campground begins to gnaw at your confidence and you start wondering when it will happen again.

At times like these, it's worth calling it a day if you can. If it's too early to stop, take a coffee break or just slow down to admire the view; take time off to study your map and you should find your usual enthusiasm returning; make that call home and boast a little about your exploits so far. When you return to your bike, you'll probably find you are quite your old self again, excited by the prospect of covering new ground, confident that you can cope with whatever comes your way. Touring alone is not always easy, but the rewards are many. You feel so aware of the places you travel through, you notice more than usual, you can absorb more of the ambience and feel at one with your surroundings. You will usually meet more people when traveling alone.

Female Passengers

My early touring days were spent on the back of my boyfriend's bikes; first a Yamaha 250, then an XS11, a Yamaha 650 and finally, real luxury, a BMW 600. All the same boyfriend, fortunately, since he changed bikes more often than girlfriends!

Passengering can be a really enjoyable experience, providing you have absolute confidence in your pilot. This is very important, particularly if you are planning to tour for long distances with this rider. Go for several shorter rides with your potential touring companion before you jump behind him and set off on a long trip. Days and days spent cringing behind a daredevil rider isn't my idea of fun and you could well

Not too long ago, a woman's "rightful" place in the motorcycling world was considered to be on the pillion seat—but those days are gone forever. Even so, it's a rare male who'll make the switch from pilot to passenger with a smile on his face, so a wise female should choose her partner accordingly.

end up in a hospital bed instead of that idyllic setting you had in mind. Unfortunately, there are a lot of irresponsible riders—less so possibly among the touring fraternity— and the mildest-mannered guy can turn out to be a crazy rider. So be forewarned.

It is surprising the number of men who swear they would never travel as a passenger with a lady rider. Their objections seem to have something to do with that all too delicate male ego, and it can be a very difficult psychological problem to overcome. An English gentleman telephoned me recently to say his wife had been "nagging him" to go for a ride on her bike and what did I think? "Well, what's the problem?" I asked him. "I'd feel so silly," he told me. "What if any of my friends or neighbors saw me?" This seems to be a fairly common problem and if you are setting off on a long tour as passenger, with hopes of taking the controls at some point, you'd better be sure before you set out that your touring partner doesn't have any hang-ups about allowing a woman at the helm.

A passenger has some rights and many responsibilities. You are literally putting your life in someone else's hands and it doesn't hurt to make them aware of it. If you are new to motorcycling it is perfectly reasonable for you to expect a little extra consideration, so if you are scared, say so, and insist on slowing down until you gain confidence. I always used to think the guys I rode with were leaning much farther into curves than I ever did, but having scraped a few sidestands and footpegs myself, it began to occur to me that perhaps the passenger gets an exaggerated impression of the angle of the bike. The more I rode on the back, the more convinced I became that tight curves can be infinitely more terrifying for the passenger than the rider, another very good reason for insisting on a little extra caution from your rider, if only to keep your nerves intact. However, it is also a good reason for not panicking when you are on the back seat. If you know your rider and can trust his judgment, then let him get on with the job of riding, even if it means occasionally gritting your teeth or gripping the sides of the bike. One of the worst passengers I ever had insisted on hanging on to me, even though I pointed out some substantial grabrails on the bike. He would dig his nails into my sides whenever I attacked a curve with anything like normal zeal. I was riding well within my limits and the limits of the bike and doing my best *not* to scare my passenger. These often painful digs served only to distract me, thus putting us both at additional risk.

If you are the passenger, I suggest touring with someone who has infinite patience and understanding, because that's one thing you will both need at some time or other during the journey! There's little doubt it is more physically demanding to be the rider, but there's equally little doubt that it can get very tiring and very boring to be a passenger on the back of a motorcycle. There are also times as a passenger when you start wishing you hadn't had that extra cup of coffee and the need to find a restroom becomes an all-consuming desire—even though your partner may just be starting to thoroughly enjoy those twists and curves and the freedom of the motorcycle. Since no suspension protects a full bladder, there is no choice: you'll have to ask to stop. Don't feel too bad about it; it's easy to get reabsorbed in the motorcycle once you set off again.

Motorcycles are becoming more comfortable, especially the touring models; but even so, you will inevitably feel the need to stretch and change your seating position from time to time. Regular stops are often the answer, but if that doesn't suit your schedule it is probably as well to sort out some sort of code with your rider that warns him you are about to shift position. Several years ago I took a motorcycling colleague to the Elephant Rally, held in February at the Nurbërgring in Germany. We both had newspaper deadlines to meet, so although the weather conditions called for regular stops, we felt we had to press on. Almost numb with cold and thoroughly exhausted from a long weekend of difficult riding, we hurtled down the autobahn to catch the only ferry that would get us back in time. Suddenly my 750 Kawasaki started to handle strangely and it was all I could do to hold on to it. It took me several seconds before I realized what was causing the problem—my passenger was having a stretch and, since he was almost twice my weight, it was having a dramatic effect on the bike's handling. At the next fuel stop I told him he was to warn me if he was going to need to stretch again and we settled on a signaling system that I have used successfully many times since—one firm tap on my left shoulder for moving about on the back of the bike, one tap on my right shoulder for needing to stop when convenient, and frantic tapping on my right shoulder if I'm to stop immediately. Intercom systems have eliminated the need for such primitive communication systems for many riders, but for anyone who does not use an intercom, it is definitely worth working out some satisfactory signals before you set off.

Touring as a passenger has several advantages over touring as a rider. It can be very relaxing to just sit back and watch the world go by. You will see more of the scenery, for the road in front of you is not your responsibility and you will usually have enough energy left at the end of the day to be able to enjoy exploring your new surroundings. However, it can also be quite demanding at times, especially if the conditions are bad. You may have to sit for what seems like an eternity, feeling cold, wet, uncomfortable and thoroughly miserable. Many passengers invent mental games to keep their minds occupied, either with vehicle license plates or other objects on the road. I prefer to daydream, to mentally design completely waterproof riding gear or compose feature articles in my head. (Sadly, these words of wisdom are usually forgotten by the time we stop.) I sometimes even manage to doze off. The latter is not to be entirely recommended unless you are pretty firmly wedged in by your luggage and riding partner, but it can be a pleasant escape, providing you don't sleep too soundly and your rider is accustomed to a nodding passenger. Above all, if the conditions are really bad, give full consideration to the rider and insist on stopping if you feel *he* needs a rest. Too many riders, especially when traveling solo, continue to ride well past the stage when they are capable of functioning efficiently, and it is your responsibility as a passenger to make sure this doesn't happen, for both your sakes.

It is possible to feel excluded from the whole touring experience when you are traveling as the passenger, especially if you are fairly new to motorcycling and everyone you meet is knowledgeable about the latest models and accessories. It helps if you tour with someone who really wants to share the pleasures of motorcycling. But, even if he

Touring as a passenger can be relaxing, even boring, particularly on long stretches of highway. The passenger may want to invent mental games or indulge in some creative daydreaming; it's the passenger's responsibility to stay alert and help keep the rider alert as well.

makes you feel like an accessory of considerably less worth than the wretched machine, don't worry, it just takes time. After a few rainstorms, a breakdown or two, and some of those magic moments when the three of you are battling along the freeway or taking on sweeping curves, you'll suddenly feel that you belong, that you are not "just a passenger" but part of the touring team. It's worth waiting for, believe me.

Just a word here about clothing specifically for the passenger, although this subject will be discussed in more detail later in the chapter. In almost all cases, the passenger is at a distinct disadvantage in a motorcycle accident. Generally, the passenger seems to be catapulted farther from the motorcycle and, for this reason, it is doubly important that a passenger should always be concerned with wearing the essentials for safe riding, including a helmet, leather jacket, gloves and sturdy shoes or boots. It may be hard to put those gloves on when the temperature is in the 80s, but it's even harder coping in an accident without them.

Group Touring

Touring as part of a group seems to be something of an acquired taste. In my early days of motorcycling, I took part in several club runs, which almost invariably resulted in more time being spent at the side of the road with broken-down machines or riders who "had to have a smoke," than actually riding. I progressed to traveling to motorcycle rallies with a group of friends, but it was a slow business with bikes of varying sizes and riders of varying abilities. Eventually, I came to the conclusion it would be much more fun just to meet them there and go my own way. It was only several years later when I learned that if I was fortunate to find compatible touring companions, group touring could actually be a lot of fun.

If you are going a long way together, it is best if you all ride similar sized bikes and have compatible dining habits and life styles, at least when on the road. This is not essential, but it does make for a more enjoyable time for everyone concerned. If you really hate having to wait around for other people, if you like to get everywhere in the quickest possible time and if you really resent stopping when you could carry on, then you are probably not the ideal candidate for group touring. You will need to be flexible, accepting the fact that stopping times will be a little longer than you prefer. But you can expect a lot more laughs than you'll ever have on your own.

Finally, a word of caution. It is very easy, particularly if you are the only lady rider in the group, to be put under a lot of pressure to prove you are as good as the rest of them. You probably are, but it takes time to learn to ride well with other riders and if you are trying too hard, you won't ride even as well as usual. Don't allow yourself to feel pressured. If you are struggling to keep up, drop back and let the group know you can't go that pace just yet. The men might chalk it up to the fact that you're "only female," but that's OK. Humility hurts a lot less than taking a spill in the dirt because you overextended yourself.

Clothing For Women

Motorcycle clothing has been dealt with in the previous chapter, but since it is a

Touring with a group can be fun; but, unfortunately, there are disadvantages. One inconsiderate person, such as the rider shown here polishing his bike at a gas stop, can hold up the entire group. If you're anticipating a group tour, be prepared for this kind of holdup and include patience in your pre-tour planning.

little more tricky to find good riding attire for female motorcyclists, the topic of women's riding apparel merits further discussion. Despite an ever-growing number of women riders and passengers, it seems that surprisingly few clothing manufacturers recognize the buying potential of that segment of the riding population. Unless you are lucky enough to live near a good dealer who stocks a comprehensive range of motorcycle gear, you may feel your choice is limited to either a badly-fitting garment that barely does the job or something from an exclusive boutique that is attractive but unsuitable. You can, of course, order what you need, but from my experience, that avenue can be less than satisfactory. You will probably have a lengthy wait and in the end you will settle for whatever you get, simply to avoid having to return it and reorder.

I've made a point of complaining to manufacturers and dealers on every suitable occasion about the lack of readily-available riding gear in women's sizes. Their excuse is that not enough women ride motorcycles to make special sizes worthwhile and that the women who do ride are perfectly happy buying whatever is available. When I counter this argument by saying they probably wouldn't recognize a woman rider if they saw one, they laugh politely and change the subject. Yet it's true! I'm sure there are very few women who haven't at some time or other been mistaken for a man when they are all togged up in warm riding gear. On several occasions, at border crossings, I have been asked to remove my helmet to prove to customs officials that I really am the female pictured in my passport. I have lost count of the times I've been called "mate."

It is always a problem deciding how much importance one should place on the safety aspect of riding apparel, compared with its practicality or appearance. It makes sense to consider safety first and fashion last, but no matter how dedicated one is to motorcycling, there are times when you really hate looking an absolute sight in what you know is very "sensible" motorcycle clothing. And being forced to attend a fancy dress party looking like Charlie Chaplin in your leathers certainly doesn't help you win your argument that there is nothing "unfeminine" about riding motorcycles! Fortunately, there is a solution. Clothes suitable for motorcycling can also look good. For example, there is certainly nothing wrong with the basic idea of jeans, western shirt, T-shirt and leather jacket as suggested in the previous chapter. However, for the female touring rider, there is the additional selection of foul weather riding gear. Looks have to take a back seat when choosing wet weather attire, because fit is important for both safety and comfort. The average woman will find that her comparable size in a man's riding suit will be tight in the hips and much too large in the jacket, particularly in the shoulders. Chances are this will limit its effectiveness. Anything too tight will be colder and less water resistant, while anything that flaps around allows for drafts, as well as being distracting when riding. So, what is the answer to finding a good, warm riding suit, the essential attire of any serious touring rider? As far as women riders are concerned, it's a matter of knowing that they *are* available and that you've just got to keep on looking until you find something that really suits you. Be prepared to settle for whatever color combination is available, but make plenty of noise if there is nothing that fits you properly. It's about time women riders were recognized!

Not only does proper fit make for a better looking garment— it's less tiring and safer too. Excess material will flap in the wind, and this constant distraction is annoying as well as fatiguing to the rider.

It is also important to buy the correct gloves, especially if you are at the controls. Don't buy them too tight, particularly if you suffer from cold hands, but if they are much too big you run the risk of getting the ends of the gloves trapped under the levers as you reach for the clutch or front brake. There are gloves in ladies' sizes and some of them are very well made. However, be sure they are of the same quality as the men's version, for all too often they are scaled-down in thickness as well as size. Finding the right helmet is less of a problem, since there is now a wide variety of styles on the market. Almost all helmets are sized from extra large to extra small.

Boots are also fairly easy to obtain now that many of the fashionable styles are sturdy enough for motorcycle use. Stay away from the lightweight dress boots. They don't offer the degree of protection needed and they won't stand up well to hard use. Western boots are a good choice, if you like them, and these are widely available in western shops. Since they are also suitable for general use, you can get maximum value from them. There are also a great many hiking and climbing boots that will adequately double as motorcycle boots. Most important, they should cover the ankle, preferably by six inches or more. Leather is by far the sturdiest boot material. Some boots are designed specifically for women motorcyclists, and these are certainly worth considering if you can locate a manufacturer that makes them. While they sometimes leave a little to be desired as far as fashion is concerned, they are often a better buy than men's motorcycle boots. Since this type of boot has been designed specifically with the rider in mind, it will feature covered zippers and a sturdy sole, plus an extra layer of leather across the front of the foot to protect against the gear lever—all the little niceties that fashion boot manufacturers naturally overlook.

Well-styled and proper-fitting leathers can be among the most attractive and flattering of all motorcycle attire. There's a lot to be said for the custom-made garments, especially for full leathers, but it's also possible to find well-tailored jackets and jeans straight off the rack in both men's and women's sizes. Be a bit wary about paying too much attention to current fashion trends when buying leathers since they are an expensive item and, unless you are on an unlimited budget, are likely to be a part of your riding wardrobe for a long time. Of course, it's possible to have them altered when styles change, but this can be costly. It makes more sense to be slightly conservative in your original choice.

Some women new to motorcycling may be concerned about the effect of hours spent in the elements with only a visor to protect their good looks. Have you ever seen an outdoor enthusiast with a sallow complexion? You will need to pay particular attention to your skin when motorcycle touring but, in my experience, the fresh air is likely to do more good than harm. Arm yourself with a good bottle of moisturizing cream, whatever your skin type, and use it liberally on your face before and after a day's riding. Make sure it has soaked in well before setting off, however, or you're likely to attract more road grime than usual. A good sunscreen is also important to avoid sun and wind burn. Your face will get surprisingly dirty when riding. I recommend using a deep skin cleanser at least twice a day, but I have found the convenient wipes and cleansing tissues to be a little too strong for my face. If you don't use lipstick, be sure to use some type of lip protection as your lips are vulnerable to the drying and chapping effects of the wind. Beauty experts may well disagree with some of this advice and, if you already have a good face cleansing program, stick with it. However, the above works well for me and if your usual routine is soap and water, I'd recommend that you do a little more than that while motorcycle touring.

Your hands, too, will require extra attention, particularly if you've been riding in bad weather. Carry a tube of hand cream where it's easily accessible and use it often, or you are likely to end up with dry and often badly chapped hands, even with the protection of good gloves. If you wear make-up, make sure it is waterproof before setting out on a long run, particularly if it's likely to rain. This sounds like obvious advice, but you wouldn't believe the number of women who either forget or ignore it and end up with streaky mascara and multi-colored cheeks.

Finally, once you're satisfied that you've done your best with your motorcycle wardrobe and you've selected your essential beauty products, go enjoy yourself. Forget about taking all those "might be nice" items. There's no room for them on a motorcycle and chances are you won't want them anyway. This includes your handbag, so often stuffed full of things you rarely need. Try to do without it. You've plenty of pockets on your riding suit for your money and documents, although I'd suggest you keep them in plastic bags just in case. If you really need a little bag to carry, a leather or nylon belt pouch will do very well. Nylon pouches can be found at most any camping supply store.

Some women always manage to look good and immaculately turned out even after a day's ride in bad weather. If you're not one of them, don't worry; it's perfectly acceptable not to look your very best when touring! There are more important things to life than always having your hair well combed—and motorcycle touring is your key to that discovery.

Chapter 7
What To Take

As the departure date of your long-planned trip draws near, excitement and anticipation build. In this emotion-charged state, you must select everything you will need on your trip. It's no wonder most riders go overboard and take too much gear on the first few trips. It's an easy trap to fall into; one where you say to yourself, "I *might* need this," or "I *might* want that." The key word is "might"—strike it from your vocabulary for the purpose of selecting what to take along on a motorcycle tour. It causes nothing but problems. Instead, substitute the question, "Do I really need this?" If your mode of transportation were a pickup truck or car, your selection would be more flexible. But part of the appeal of motorcycle travel is the imposition of stringent weight and space limitations. Motorcycle touring requires the rather precise selection of equipment needed for comfortable travel.

In this chapter we will examine the different items that will be useful to the touring rider and point out some of the areas where many riders carry too much. While no elaborate checklists will be offered, the chapter goes into quite a bit of detail for the different categories of items. Each rider will have to develop his own list of items to take, based on individual requirements. Items an inexperienced rider might tend to overlook will be mentioned, and there will be suggestions on how to limit what you take. Weight and space limitations are both critical factors, but there is also the actual loading and unloading of the bike to keep in mind. You will be packing and unpacking your bike over and over again on most trips—so why make it any more difficult and time-consuming than necessary? I recall an early tour when all my gear had to be packed exactly right or valuable items wouldn't fit. As a result, the saddlebags had to be repacked several times after each overnight stop. It was not an enjoyable task.

We can separate touring gear into two major categories: those items that will be used on the bike and those for off-bike use. There will be considerable overlapping of items with a dual function. Multiple-use items are the most desirable, as they allow you to carry less. Although we have discussed riding clothes in depth in Chapter 5, the following list will indicate how many of these items will also fall under the heading of off-bike use. (The items that will serve a dual role are flagged with an asterisk.)

Helmet, glasses*, jacket*, gloves, jeans*, boots* and T-shirt* comprise the basic riding outfit for hot weather. Sunglasses also fit into the dual-purpose category, as does a leather jacket. Other clothing requirements consist of a long-sleeved, western-style cotton shirt*, sweater*, leather chaps, electric vest* and electric chaps, and rain gear, including a rainsuit*, rubber overboots and rain mitts. About the only other item needed for most summer tours will be a heavier pair of gloves.

Many riders will find that no other off-bike wear is required, although each individual should evaluate his own needs for the tour, considering weather, recreational activities and personal dress requirements. A rider planning to stay a few days at a hotel in New Orleans or Las Vegas will have different clothing requirements than the rider whose plans include backpacking in Glacier National Park. But if no special activities are planned, the basic wardrobe outlined above will serve quite nicely for off-bike wear if you add the items needed for changes (extra underclothes, socks and handkerchiefs).

Take clothing in a variety of weights rather than simply duplicate items. For instance, I might carry two or three long-sleeved cotton shirts, but all will be different weights; a very light one and a moderately heavy fabric (I'm partial to the blue denim material for this weight). If I'm expecting cool or cold weather, I will add a third heavyweight shirt. If I carry an extra pair of jeans, I'll select an older and a newer pair. Since repeated washings tend to lighten jeans, in weight as well as color, the older ones will be the coolest for really hot days. If for some reason I need to dress up on a trip, I will substitute a pair of dress slacks for the second pair of jeans, add a dress shirt and, on very rare occasions, include a necktie (some finer restaurants require it). With this outfit and a cardigan-style sweater doubling as a sport jacket, I can dress comfortably for just about any situation.

If camping and/or hiking is planned during hot weather, a pair of walking shorts can be substituted for the second pair of jeans—with the only other off-bike addition possibly being a swimsuit. This may constitute a meager travel wardrobe for many people, but it's amazing just how much latitude your clothing choices offer. Length of trip plays almost no part in the selection of what to wear. A very long trip doesn't call for packing any more clothes than a trip of a few days. With the sweater and different styles of shirts (long-sleeved cotton and T-shirts with a pocket), you can vary your dress to adapt to almost any temperature or type of activity. With the addition of jacket, vest or rainsuit top (used as a light windbreaker off the bike), there are many clothing combinations.

Additional footwear poses a bit of a problem, partly because shoes or extra boots are quite bulky to pack, but activities such as jogging or hiking may require special footwear. If no activities are planned, extra footwear really isn't required, but it is rather restful to be able to change into a different pair of shoes after wearing riding boots all day. Hard-soled moccasins have proven to be a good choice; they are easy to pack and feel almost like wearing slippers in the motel room or campsite, yet they are suitable for short walks. An excellent footwear choice is sneakers or running shoes, as they are quite versatile, especially for camping. I find pull-on or zippered riding boots suitable for nearly any type of off-bike wear, including wear with dress slacks. Obviously, there are many items of dress that can be used for motorcycle travel that are not listed here, but you will need to apply fairly strict limitations to what you take.

The next category is loosely termed "travel accessories." Included are items strictly for bike maintenance as well as those used by the rider.

Logbook. A logbook is a notebook used for recording various items concerning the bike, including a record of gasoline purchases noting mpg figures and where the fuel was purchased. Some riders include a trip diary in their logbooks, chronicling their experiences on the road for interesting reading later. It is also helpful to log photograph-taking in a diary, simplifying identification of people and places. I use the logbook to record tread depth on the tires every 500 miles and to note the weight of touring gear carried.

Tools. I carry a six-inch adjustable wrench and a screwdriver. (I like the type of screwdriver some motorcycle manufacturers supply with their tool kits, with a shaft that has a bladed tip on one end and a Phillips tip on the other.) The wrench and screwdriver are auxiliary to the motorcycle tool kit. I carry the wrench and screwdriver in the tank bag or fairing, where they are easily accessible. The tool kit is generally stored under the seat and is more difficult to get at. Ease of accessibility applies to chain lube, as well. Keep it in a handy location, so when the chain is still warm at a fuel, meal or overnight stop, it's easy to lube the chain and check for proper adjustment.

I like the idea of a tire repair kit, but have stopped using one, partly because I take very good care of my tires and change them when they wear down to $2/32$-inch tread depth. I carry a tread depth gauge and air pressure gauge. As mentioned, the tread depth is measured every 500 miles or so. I also visually inspect both front and rear tires for any type of damage. By reading tread depth, you can determine tire wear and plan for replacements when needed. Consequently, I don't have many flats. But I have found very few places in this country where one couldn't get a tire repaired. I carried a tire repair kit for years, along with a spare inner tube. In fact, I wore out that inner tube, packing it around on so many trips. I finally cut it up into rubber bands and got far more use out of it that way. However, if you feel safer or more secure with a tire repair kit, by all means carry one.

I adjust tire pressures according to load, using the manufacturer's recommendations. In general, the two-up rider with loaded saddlebags and gear attached to the luggage rack will be at or near the maximum allowable weight, so the rear tire pressure can be raised to its maximum rated pressure. Proper rear tire inflation in conjunction with adequate rear suspension will go a long way toward making a heavily loaded bike more comfortable and manageable.

Spare parts. Motorcycle spares fall pretty much into the same category as tire repair kits; they can be nice to have, but rarely turn out to be necessary. The exceptions are fuses and light bulbs, especially if the bulbs used on your bike aren't always readily available at service stations. Quartz headlight bulbs fall into the category of being hard to find, but—fortunately—they are lightweight and easy to pack. The only precaution is to be sure to protect them against breakage. Most late-model bikes will have one or

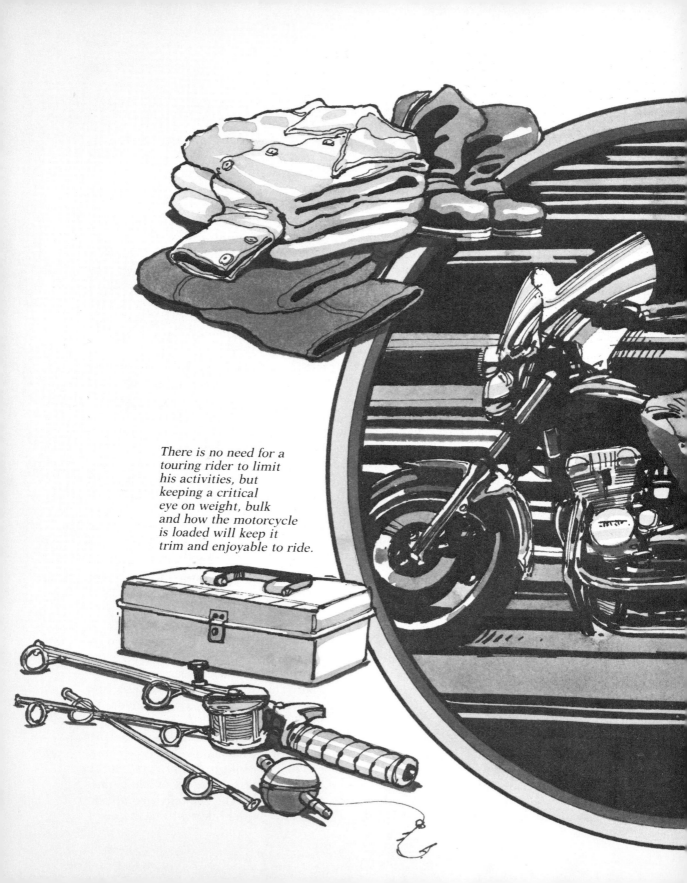

There is no need for a
touring rider to limit
his activities, but
keeping a critical
eye on weight, bulk
and how the motorcycle
is loaded will keep it
trim and enjoyable to ride.

two spare fuses in the fuse box, but if not provided, at least one spare of each size should be packed. One other popular spare part for a motorcycle is an extra clutch cable. It is possible to ride without a clutch (if the cable is broken), but not very pleasant when stopping and starting. A spare cable can be coiled and packed in the headlight nacelles behind the reflector, or simply taped to the outside of the installed clutch cable.

A couple of small items that prove quite useful for making minor repairs are a roll of plastic electrical tape and a small roll (about the size of a half dollar) of wire. In the long run, however, the very best protection against breakdowns and equipment failures is proper maintenance and lubrication. Both will go a long way toward eliminating any need for spare parts or roadside repairs.

Maps and tour guides. I especially like the oil company state maps. They offer a wealth of detail that can provide useful information for a day's touring, such as locations of campsites, mountain passes and the tiniest towns—information that is frequently lacking on larger scale maps. The Automobile Association of America (AAA) offers tour guides that are an excellent source of information for the touring rider. If storage space is especially critical, these guides can be cut apart, leaving only the information required for a particular tour. These guides frequently cover several states in one volume, so if information is only needed for one or two states, the rest can be left at home. A list of addresses and phone numbers of friends and relatives can prove handy to have along.

Other small items I find useful are pre-soaked towelettes, a small packet of facial tissue, suntan lotion and a small water bottle. I like to keep at least a pint of water on the bike—especially for desert riding—but it's nice to have along anytime. I recommend a first aid kit—one that is totally personalized. Such things as aspirin and Band-Aids are frequently all that will be needed, but if you regularly use certain products or prescriptions, include them, as well. Sporting goods stores generally offer some really compact first aid kits that will easily fit in a pocket and can be adapted to meet your personal needs. This brings up a point that applies to first aid, as well as a great many other things. Touring in the United States, you are never far from some form of civilization. Any need that arises on a trip can usually be attended to at the nearest town, whether you have an upset stomach, a head cold or need to replace a lost or damaged item. Knowing this, you should feel somewhat confident that everything you might need on a trip doesn't have to be carried along. Take only what you will actually need— the "might need" items will take care of themselves. I will suggest a "might be handy" item that turns out to be useful in many instances. Generally associated with camping, a Swiss army knife packs small and will serve a number of purposes. The knife I carry has a scissors, tweezers, can opener, bottle opener, large and small screwdriver blades, plus several other small tools.

Personal items. Each rider will want to pack some form of cleanup or toilet kit, but it should be kept as simple and compact as personal requirements permit. The travel kit I carry is the size of a carton of cigarettes. Most toilet articles, like toothpaste and after-shave lotion, are available in small containers or can be transferred to smaller plastic bottles. If you camp, a bar of soap and towel must be included in your kit, but these aren't necessary for the motel user.

Sports and hobby equipment. Here is an area with a great deal of variability that will differ considerably for each rider and each tour. Probably the most common item in this category is camera gear. Photography equipment can be as simple or comprehensive as one's skill and interest dictate. The basic kit will include a camera and several rolls of film (remember that film is sold in all parts of the country). The pocket-size cameras using cartridge film are popular for snapshots, but even the more sophisticated models are small enough to carry comfortably. The 35mm camera equipment will give better quality pictures, plus a wider selection of equipment. There are some very fine, very compact 35mm range-finder cameras on the market now, some rivaling pocket cameras in size. If the camera you select has a self-timed shutter release, use of a tiny tripod will allow the photographer to be in some of the photos, as well. For the serious photo hobbiest, the single lens reflex camera in the 35mm format is hard to beat. These models offer all the latest features, in addition to interchangeable lenses. I use one of the very smallest 35mm SLRs with automatic exposure and a 28 to 85mm zoom lens and find it an incredibly versatile piece of equipment for touring purposes. Single lens reflex cameras are more expensive and do require a certain amount of care in packing and handling.

Beyond photography, we get into rather specialized categories of sports or hobby equipment, but a few areas are popular enough to mention. Hiking and backpacking are growing in popularity among all age groups, and for many riders, these activities fit in well with touring and camping. In addition, the equipment is versatile enough to be fully integrated into a motorcycle touring outfit. For instance, hiking boots are available that fill both backpacking and motorcycling needs. Many of these boots are listed as hunting models, with sturdy lug soles and lace-up tops that come well above the ankles. There are backpacks that can be substituted for duffle bags and much motorcycle camping gear will be found in a backpacker's catalog.

Fishing is a sport that goes very nicely with the basic outdoor nature of touring. Here again, you can turn to the backpacker catalog to find equipment suitable for fishing, especially fishing rods. Multi-piece backpacking-style rods are available in a wide range of styles and prices, and their short, packed size, 20 to 35 inches in most cases, makes them relatively easy to carry on the bike. The best models will have fiberglass ferrules (bands that connect the separate rod pieces), rather than metal ones. The metal types work fine, but fiberglass makes for much better fishing action. I limit my fishing gear to freshwater tackle for motorcycle touring, because it's the most compact. But a medium-weight, six- to seven-foot spinning rod and a lightweight open-face spinning reel form a versatile outfit for fishing from a boat, a lakeshore or stream-bank. A few hooks, a packet or two of split-shot sinkers, some spinner and spoon lures (all in a hip-pocket-size tackle box) will get the job done in most situations. But, here again, most fishing areas will have tackle or bait shops where the local specialty lure can be purchased, and these places are a good source of information on where, when and how the local fish are being caught. For the dedicated trout fisherman, a fly rod (or combination fly and spinning rod) can be substituted along with the appropriate

It isn't always the female half of a riding couple who wants to take too much on a tour. But often the less experienced rider is inclined to select too much gear.

HIS
COMMON
HERS

reel and other tackle. If I anticipate much stream fishing, I will find room for a light-weight pair of stocking foot waders and use them with a pair of canvas sneakers. As with all other items to be carried, weight and size must be balanced against need and frequency of use.

About the only other major category of touring gear is camping equipment. An entire chapter has been devoted to camping, so suggestions on what to carry are discussed there.

How To Pack

One of the problems that can arise for two-up touring riders is the division of storage space. A simple solution, and a common one, is the allotment of one saddlebag per person for personal items. Here is one suggestion on how to keep peace in the family. The packing method calls for two identical cardboard boxes (apple crates do nicely), plus a third box of the same size or larger. Label them respectively, "his," "hers," and "common." While most items will fall naturally into one of the three categories, others will be in somewhat of a "gray" area. Most camping gear will go into the common box, including cooking gear. One rule that seems to help is that anything going into the common box must be agreed upon by both riders; if not, it goes into the personal box of the one who wants it included. If you can keep this whole process from getting too serious, it can be both fun and helpful in keeping overall weight to a minimum. It's an easy matter to weigh the boxes on a bathroom scale when they are empty, and to keep track of how much weight each person is accumulating by weighing the box of gear when it is full. Adding these figures will give a fair idea of what the total weight will be when the bike is loaded for the trip. It also makes a rather convenient way to store things between trips, especially the specialized items that are needed only for touring.

The box concept works well with or without checklists. In some respects, the box itself functions as a checklist, allowing one to view everything selected at one time. But a checklist can be taped to the box and items marked off as they go into the box for those who prefer some way to keep a record of what is being packed. Checklists are normally thought of as a way to keep from forgetting items, but they can be doubly useful if each rider will make a thoughtful list of things to take, asking himself for each item, "Do I really need this?" Use the checklist to limit what is taken and as a reminder list for items to bring.

While there have been repeated references to taking less in this chapter, no real optional solutions have been offered for the situations where certain items are quite important to the trip, but are impossible to take along. I frequently use one alternative that works rather well. It does require a little planning and forethought, but can pay off by assuring you will have exactly what you need without overloading the bike. Shipping a box of items via UPS or parcel post is one way of getting your gear where you want it without having to exceed your motorcycle GVWR. I try to take at least one major trip to the Northwest every year for steelhead fishing. This kind of fishing doesn't lend itself to motorcycle touring, yet I usually make the trip by bike. Steelhead fishing requires gear that isn't available in the take-apart style, plus quite a bit of heavy, specialized clothing, like insulated foot waders or hip boots. A week or two before the trip, I box everything up and send it to my fishing friend in Washington state. It helps if you have a specific address to ship to, although you can use general delivery. This method also works with special clothing, like dress clothes for business purposes, a wedding or a special function you want to attend while on tour. Incidentally, this also works very nicely the other way around. If you find items on the trip that you must have, but can't carry on your bike, simply package them up and ship or mail them back to yourself at home.

In general, selecting what to take is a matter of deciding what's really necessary and practicing a fair degree of restraint in your choices. I appreciate that this will vary considerably among riders. I know one couple who think "roughing it" on overnight stops means having to stay in a motel with only black and white TV, so their idea of a minimum wardrobe varies considerably from the thinking of most touring riders. When it comes to making final decisions on what to take, each person should keep in mind his reasons for touring, and what he wants to get out of a particular tour—then make a selection of gear accordingly.

Chapter 8
Camping

Most of us spend the major part of our adult lives indoors—it's where we sleep, eat, work and play—unless we make a real effort to take some of our activities out-of-doors. This is part of the appeal of motorcycling. It takes us out into the fresh air and, coupled with touring and camping, helps to bring us back in tune with Mother Nature.

Camping is by no means a mandatory part of motorcycle touring, but the two activities complement each other extremely well. There's something quite special about setting off on a trip, your camping gear neatly stowed on the back of your motorcycle. It gives you that rare feeling of freedom and independence—the confidence of knowing that you are ready for anything the world can throw at you. Suddenly your motorcycle has been transformed into a magic carpet that can take you anywhere you want to go.

Back to earth, and from the practical point of view, camping offers a fairly economical way of getting about the country. Overnight accommodations and meals are probably the two biggest cost items when traveling, especially for two-up riders, so it's worth looking at ways of keeping costs within reason.

I consider I have three, or perhaps four, options on overnight accommodations. At the top of the price list is a motel or hotel room; much farther down the scale is a campground; then there is a free camp at the side of the road, or, if you are lucky, you can beg a room with friends or relatives, the only price being a gift for whoever you are visiting. So let us look at the advantages and disadvantages of the four choices.

Motel or hotel stops are a convenient and comfortable option, but obviously you are going to have to pay—sometimes dearly. Prices start at around $12 a night, but you can pay $50 or more. On the average, you can figure on paying about $15 minimum for one person, or $20 for two. There is also a small cost to your time schedule, since it is advisable to check in by 3 to 6 p.m., especially for the less expensive motels.

While it is sometimes possible to do a limited amount of cooking in your room, it is often against the regulations and is not to be recommended at any time. You may decide to have restaurant meals, but in this case you need to allow about $12 to $15 per person per day, which considerably increases the cost of your motel stop.

It can be fun to drop in on friends or relatives, but there are drawbacks. Few of them will live at convenient stopping places along your planned route, so at best you will have to make several detours. Often it will mean spending more time than you can really afford in order to make the visit worthwhile, so your day's mileage is sure to be affected. I find the easiest solution is to make phone calls or short visits to friends and relatives along the way and to sort out my overnight accommodations independently.

This brings us to camping, both in established campgrounds and at impromptu locations. Campgrounds will range in price from no-charge to $10 a night. On the average, you can expect to pay about $4 a night.

Among my favorite campgrounds are those on national forest land and, often being very primitive, they are usually quite cheap. Most expensive are the privately owned, luxury camping resorts that provide a wide range of facilities, including modern rest rooms and showers, recreation rooms, swimming pools and tennis courts. Some will even offer specialized activities such as horseback riding, boating and fishing.

Somewhere between these two extremes are the state and federal parks. These are by far the most commonly available and, in most cases, they offer good value for the money. They usually cost $3 to $4 a day, and for this you nearly always get showers and flush toilets, plus the many facilities you would expect in a park built with public funds, such as swimming, hiking trails and numerous other recreational opportunities.

Whatever type of campground you choose, you will usually find your site has its own picnic table and firepit, a trash can nearby and a supply of drinking water. It is normally possible to park your bike close to the tent.

Firewood is almost always available. In the most primitive campgrounds, you may be able to gather your own firewood free of charge, but in the parks and resorts, you usually have to buy it by the bundle if you want an open fire.

Let us now make a rough calculation of how much can be saved by choosing to camp rather than relying on motel stops all the time. Since we are working on averages, we can estimate spending $4 a night for the campground plus about $5 per person per day for food from the market. This may sound a little high, but there is the problem of having to shop in small out-of-the-way places where prices will undoubtedly be higher, as well as having to buy in lesser quantities which tends to be more expensive.

From this, we can see that a solo rider who stays in motels and eats in restaurants can expect to spend around $25 to $30 a day, whereas camping and cooking will cost less than $10 a day. This is a difference of about $120 a week. For the touring couple, the difference can be even greater. Their motel and restaurant bills will total about $45 to $50 daily, whereas campsites and food cost a total of $15 at the most—a weekly difference of over $200!

Obviously, this budgeting is rather general and subject to individual requirements, but it does indicate the importance of looking closely at your food and shelter if you are trying to keep costs low. It is also clear that it would not take many weeks on the road to offset the cost of even the most elaborate camping equipment. It is easy to see why camping is so popular with touring riders, especially for anyone traveling on a budget.

Later in this chapter we will explore the various types of camping gear in the different price ranges, while in Chapter 13 we will take a closer look at figuring out travel costs. Right now we are considering whether or not to camp, so let's look at some of the possible drawbacks.

In general, it is fairly simple to find a campground that suits you since most areas of the United States are liberally sprinkled with them, both public and privately owned. Books are available listing all these campgrounds, but on the whole, they are too thick and heavy to take with you on the bike. They can be useful if you want to select a few campgrounds before you leave home, but I prefer to rely on oil company maps which show the majority of public campgrounds, usually indicated by a pine tree symbol or a triangle.

Most of the time you should have little difficulty getting into the campground of your choice, but there are certain areas and times of the year when you could run into problems.

Seashore and national parks are among the most desirable campgrounds, and these fill up quite early in the day, especially in high season and on weekends. If you partic-

The touring rider has a virtually limitless selection of campsites to choose from.

Most riders feel more comfortable with the bike parked so it's visible from the tent.

ularly want to camp in this type of campground during the peak summer months, you should start looking before noon and be prepared to settle for a second or third choice.

Even campgrounds that have a reservation system will frequently set aside a few sites on a first-come basis, so an early stop can get you in at one of these. If your plans call for several nights in a particular campground, it would be advisable to try to make a reservation before you start the trip. Generally, I avoid making any reservations, preferring a more relaxed schedule, but this can often mean having to look elsewhere when my favorite site is filled.

Campsites near metropolitan areas are scarce, and the few that are available are generally overcrowded, especially on holiday weekends. Those near famous landmarks or in popular vacation areas, as well as those easily accessible from well-traveled highways, can also be difficult to get into, unless you are very lucky.

One easy answer is to stop fairly early in the day, preferably before 4 p.m. in the majority of places. Chances are you will get in at your first choice of campground but, if not, there is still plenty of time to find an acceptable alternative.

When things get really desperate, you still have the option of camping in any out-of-the-way place you can find. It is by no means ideal, but it can work. There are many disadvantages, not the least of which is the risk of being routed out during the night by the law or an angry landowner, which can be unpleasant and embarrassing. In addition, it is not always safe, especially if you are on your own, as you may well be harassed by someone who decides you are a stranger to the place and therefore easy prey.

Another disadvantage of an impromptu site is the lack of facilities. It is difficult to manage for long without a fresh water supply, and with no toilets, fireplace or picnic table, even the most idyllic spot will quickly lose its charm. It is best to use such spots as places for a short night's sleep and to be back on the road at first light.

Having said all that, I must admit there are times when this sort of campsite seems the simplest solution. However, I have my own set of rules, acquired over the years, for use when selecting a suitable place to pitch my tent. The most important of these is to get out of sight of the road. This considerably improves the odds against being disturbed.

The land adjacent to creeks, rivers, lakes and even oceans will often provide suitable sites for this kind of overnight stop, and these can sometimes be very attractive, despite the lack of amenities. The desert is another area that lends itself to this type of camping, even though it is not always the most inviting. It is usually possible to find a track leading off the main road into some quiet, secluded spot.

National and state forests often provide plenty of suitable sites (in other than established campgrounds), but here any form of fire is out since it will almost certainly be prohibited.

The really dedicated camper can usually find a suitable campsite anywhere, but there are some places that don't easily lend themselves to camping. For example, you are wasting your time looking around a major metropolitan area within reasonable distance of the city center. Indeed, if you find yourself in this sort of location, too tired to ride any farther, you'd do well to consider paying for a night's lodging. There are one or two other occasions when a motel stop is by far the most attractive option. After a week or so in a tent, it can seem a real treat to have all the luxury and privacy of a motel room—an abundance of hot water and clean towels. What bliss!

For this reason, I try to make every fifth night or so a motel stop. If it is planned into the budget, you have no need to consider the extra cost, unless you have already had a lot of unexpected expenses. It is good to have a break from the rigors of camping, and it will make the following night in the tent all the more pleasurable.

Hopefully, by now you are convinced about the merits of camping and, if so, you will want to know what equipment to select. It can be fun choosing your new camping gear, and it makes sense to get it right, since it will play such a big part in the trip. Don't try to "make do" with equipment unsuited to motorcycle use, as it will prove almost impossible to load well and could ruin your riding experience.

Motorcycle camping gear is pretty basic, but nonetheless it is specialized equipment and is not always available at every sporting goods or hardware store. Most suitable gear will be labeled "backpacker equipment" and is stocked at specialty stores. Since most of these are in metropolitan areas, we have included a list of catalog suppliers at the end of this chapter for anyone who needs an alternative source.

As with everything else for the touring rider, camping equipment must be judged quite severely on its weight and bulk; obviously, the lighter and smaller, the better.

I remember the first time I saw a real backpacker tent. Of course, I had seen them in catalogs and read the figures, but that did not have nearly the impact of holding the little nylon and aluminum bundle in my hand (it weighed about 6½ pounds). It was only about 10 or 11 pounds lighter than the tent I had been using, but the difference in bulk was incredible. It was even more surprising when I set both tents up, for the little backpacking model was actually more spacious inside and included a rain flysheet in its tiny package. The only drawback was its price, since it cost nearly three times as much as the heavier model.

That was a few years ago, and since then there have been big improvements in both design and materials for lightweight tents, so the choice is much greater and prices more realistic. There really is no need to use up your weight allowance with just the tent, but you must be prepared to pay if you want one of the very lightest models. Lightweight, quality equipment is very expensive, but it can be a good investment if it is going to get a lot of use.

If I had to settle for a single item for camping, it would be a good sleeping bag. A good night's sleep is important for any touring rider, and there is no reason why you should lose out just because you choose to camp. It doesn't have to be the most expensive sleeping bag on the market, but you do need to know what you are looking for and to keep in mind the use it is going to have. If you are touring in the summer, you could be uncomfortably warm in some of the top-range bags.

For general use, select a sleeping bag suitable for relatively mild temperatures (unless you are particularly cold-blooded!), from about 40 degrees to about 10 or 15 degrees above zero. Most bags in this category will be labeled for "three-season" use or, if a minimum temperature range is used, they will be the ones in the 10- to 20-degree range. The temperature ratings vary slightly from manufacturer to manufacturer, so just use them as a guide.

If you plan to spend a lot of time traveling in the mountains, or will be touring chiefly in the early and late season, you should consider a slightly warmer bag. Several factors affect a bag's warmth: its construction, the amount of filling, type of filling, as well as its style and size.

Let's examine some of these factors more closely, bearing in mind that the bag's overall bulk and weight are still important considerations.

Warmth is largely determined by the type and amount of filling used. Generally, the choice is between synthetic and down—the latter being preferable in most instances, but appreciably more expensive. In fact, one of the only real advantages of a synthetic filling is that, unlike down, it retains most of its insulating qualities when wet.

Goose down is one of the most popular fillings, since it has the greatest loft and temperature range of any material available, which allows it to be compressed into a much smaller package than the equivalent synthetic bag. Good quality down backpacker sleeping bags in the three-season or moderate-temperature range are priced from about $100 to $300. If price is important, the synthetic bags are worth considering as they are quite a lot cheaper. Non-backpacking styles with synthetic filling are widely

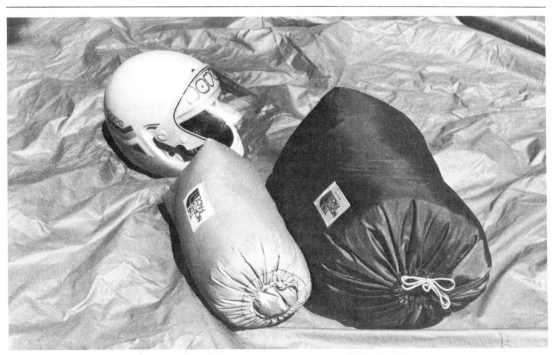

These sleeping bags illustrate the difference in size between the down-filled bag (left) and *the larger synthetic-filled bag on the right. Temperature range is almost identical.*

available and can be bought in discount stores, drug and hardware stores, as well as from most good sports dealers. They are available for less than $30 and, providing you are aware of their limitations, are perfectly usable.

The main disadvantages are that they tend to be rather bulky, considering their limited warmth, and the overall quality is low, apparent in the use of cheap zippers and sewn-through seams. Most of these bags will be made of unlabeled polyester or Holofill 808 polyester. The slightly better quality and progressively more expensive synthetic bags use Holofill II or PolarGuard as filling. These bags range from around $50 to over $100.

The best synthetic bags share many of the quality features found in down bags. These include such things as self-healing nylon coil zippers, as well as boxed or over-lapping tube designs which help keep the filling in place. One feature worth having is a hood, since it greatly contributes to warmth in bad conditions and, if it's not needed, can simply be left open. However, if a hood is missing, you may find a knitted wool watchcap works almost as well.

Backpacker-style bags come in mummy, modified mummy, semi-rectangular and rectangular shapes. Most popular among touring riders are the modified mummy and the semi-rectangular. The pure mummy is rather restrictive and is only worth considering if light weight and size are of critical importance. At the other extreme, the rectangular version is more roomy, but it doesn't pack down nearly as well as the others, regardless of fill material. The modified mummy packs smaller than the semi-rectangular, but is less convenient should you wish to zip two together to make a double bag (the zipper runs down the middle of the paired, modified mummy bags). The semi-rectangular bags open out flat and can be linked together with the zipper running around the edge. The extra length of zipper along the foot of the semi-rectangular bag also allows it to be opened slightly at the feet for added ventilation in hot weather.

Few rectangular or semi-rectangular bags are available with a hood, and they lose a little in warmth to the equivalent weight mummy, as well as being slightly bulkier when packed. For this reason, they will only be found in the lower- and middle-warmth range of the backpacker styles. These bags score highest for versatility, however, and can even be used as a comforter on the bed at home.

Ripstop nylon is the traditional material for the shell of this type of sleeping bag. Its only real disadvantage is that in hot weather it feels too warm, and in cold weather it feels wet and cold initially. Some manufacturers have tried to correct this by using a nylon-taffeta blend which, while it feels better, tends to be slightly heavier and bulkier.

If I'm using a ripstop nylon-covered bag, I take a small fitted sheet from which I've cut the top two corners. The two remaining fitted corners are placed toward the bottom of the bag and, if the sheet works its way up, I can hook a toe into each corner and realign it. The sheet adds warmth in cold weather and makes a good lightweight cover for hot weather. I also add my own trimmed-down version of a zippered pillow cover (the regular size is too big and a waste of valuable space), which I stuff with clothes to make a pillow.

Unless you are really dedicated to sleeping on the rough ground, you might like

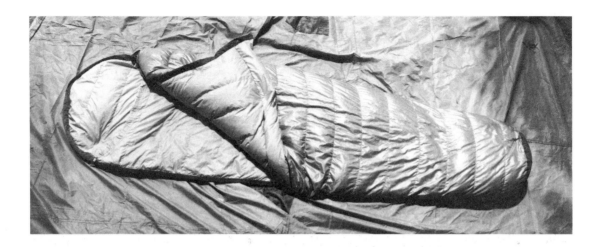

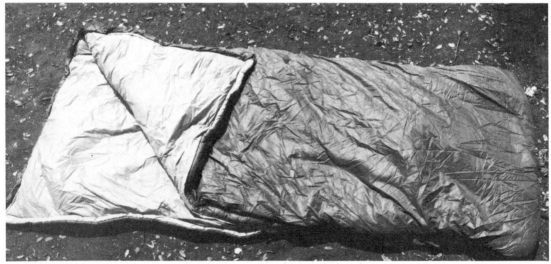

The modified mummy style sleeping bag   *The bag below is more versatile but less*
(above) features a "boxed" foot section.   *practical for touring because it's bulkier.*

to consider some form of mattress. The foam mats in the 48 x 20-inch backpacker size
are a good choice. Foam mattresses are a little bulkier than the air-filled type, but at
least they won't let you down in the middle of the night as the latter have a tendency
to do. Both types start at around $5, ranging up to around $30 for the newest self-
inflating air mattress, which, incidentally, is well worth its relatively high price.

Your choice of tent is an important one, since it is going to be your main source
of shelter—and privacy—while you are camping. I well remember one night when we
reached our destination rather late and found all the campgrounds full, so we unrolled
the sleeping bags and curled up next to the bike in a parking lot. The following morning

I woke to find myself looking directly into a stranger's eyes. He had just been curious, but I felt as though my privacy had been invaded.

In addition to a bit of privacy, your tent will offer you a lot of protection from bad weather, flying and crawling insects, snakes, or any other small creature that might be tempted to share your warm sleeping bag if you were out in the open.

When selecting your tent, you must first decide how much room you need. Ideally, you should buy a tent that is "one person" bigger than the number intending to use it. One person bigger? Tents are generally measured by the number of people they will sleep, on the basis that each person is allowed 2½ x 6½ feet of ground space.

If you are planning on strictly "one-night stands," you can probably manage with the smaller tent, but if you intend to set up camp for several days at a time, you will appreciate the extra space.

For the solo rider, the "two-man" tent is a perfect size, offering plenty of room for all the gear from the bike, while still leaving adequate sleeping space. The touring couple can probably manage quite well in the three-person size, but one of the compact four-man tents would offer a lot more comfort. This is particularly important if you

Shown above, from left to right, are two-, four-, and three-person camping tents. All feature external frames and are covered with a rain fly.

Keeping your food out of
the tent and safely tied up
in a tree will make
midnight raids from the
local bruins less traumatic.

are likely to have to cope with bad weather; the extra living space can make life a lot more bearable.

One word of warning here: bad weather and all that extra space may tempt you to do some of your cooking under canvas. This is risky and inadvisable for at least two reasons. First, there is the obvious danger of fire, however careful you try to be. Second, the odors from the cooking tend to cling to the fabric of the tent, and they could attract a most unwelcome visitor—a bear. Bears go for what smells good and, if that happens to be your tent, you might well wake up one night with an angry bruin ripping your tent apart to get at whatever is edible. For this reason, it is also wise to keep food well away from your tent. The same rules apply when there are raccoons in the area. While they are not usually dangerous, they can do a lot of damage to your expensive nylon backpacking tent if they smell food inside.

Close proximity with wild animals is one of the greatest benefits of camping. I have had deer, bears, raccoons, squirrels, chipmunks and many types of birds visit my camp-sites many times while I sat quietly and simply watched them (except for the bears). For those of us who live in towns and cities, this is a wonderful experience to be cherished and remembered.

At night or when I leave camp, I find the best way to protect my food is to string it up in a bag and hang it from a tree on a rope (nylon parachute cord works fine). For my own protection, I keep something in the tent that will make a lot of noise, such as a spoon and pot, or an empty tin can with a few small rocks inside.

Bears and raccoons have been into my saddlebags looking for food, and both have taken things from my picnic table (footprints gave them away), but they have never ventured into my tent, which I attribute to no food smells.

Two types of ripstop nylon are used for tents, one coated for waterproofing and the other uncoated. The waterproof material is used for the floor and usually extends several inches up the sidewalls to keep all ground water out. Above this is the other nylon fabric, which breathes, allowing any moisture inside the tent to escape. This is covered by a separate, waterproof rain flysheet. This type of system is light, easy to set up and works well.

Some of the latest types of tents are being fitted with Gore-Tex panels, which have the amazing property of allowing water vapor to pass freely while preventing any liquid water from getting through. Unfortunately, this material is still very expensive; otherwise it would be the near-perfect answer.

Tents most suited to the motorcyclist's needs will, once again, come from the range of backpacking equipment. Not all backpacker tents are suitable, however. Stay clear of any labeled "expeditionary" or "mountaineering," as they do not really offer the ventilation needed and are only acceptable in the extreme conditions for which they are designed. Backpacker tents come in a wide range of styles, but most can be classified as either A-frame or the slightly newer dome models. Both use external aluminum frames.

Many of the new dome-style tents are real works of art, but they tend to be expensive, and more complex than is necessary for motorcycle touring. The A-frame styles are more practical for our needs and their only real fault is the broad surface they present to strong crosswinds. However, I have experienced crosswinds up to 30 mph while using the two-man size A-frame, without damage, so it should not present too much of a problem unless you plan to be in areas of high winds regularly.

Some of the dome-style and the A-frame models are free-standing; that is, they do not require tent pegs or guy-lines—a very desirable feature. This makes them very easy to erect, and they can even be used on paved surfaces should the need arise. The other advantage is that they can easily be moved once set up, which can be useful if, for instance, you are troubled by campfire smoke blowing into the tent, or you find a root under your bed when you turn in for the night. Most of these free-standing models have provision for stakes and guy-lines, so you can fasten them down in high winds or bad weather.

Once again, size and weight are of prime importance when selecting a tent. The upper limit for weight is around 10 pounds, while 25 or 26 inches is about the longest that will pack easily on a bike.

Prices for backpacker tents vary enormously. You can spend anything from $50 to over $500, but most riders will find something suitable in the $150 to $300 range. This includes several A-frame models for two, three or four people, plus a few of the new Gore-Tex models.

Before making your final selection, check that the tents you are considering offer adequate ventilation. There should be a good air flow in at least one direction; a screened door with a screened window at the opposite end is the most common and it works well.

Set up your new tent as soon as you get it home, crawl in and out of it, inspecting it for damage or flaws in manufacturing. Check all the seams, set up your mattress and sleeping bag to see how much space is left and, finally, spray the outside of the tent with a hose to see if it leaks at all. It is far better to deal with potential problems *before* leaving home.

Next, buy a tube of sealant, if one was not supplied with the tent, and seal any seams in the floor or flysheet that looked as if they leaked.

It is a good idea to be perfectly familiar with setting up and taking down your tent before you set out, or you can guarantee that it will be dark and pouring rain the first time you have to do it!

Before closing on the subject of tents, there is one other alternative that might interest any solo rider who wants something basic and not too expensive—the bivouac sack. While it offers few of the benefits of a tent, it is a lot better than sleeping out in the open and is a practical answer if all you want is somewhere to sleep out of the rain and away from the mosquitoes. There is very little room inside—just enough for one person and a sleeping bag—but it costs about $100, is set up in an instant, is extremely light and packs up really small. Most bivouac sacks are now made in Gore-Tex, so you are almost certain to stay snug, dry and warm inside, whatever the weather conditions.

Once you have your tent, sleeping bag and mattress, you're pretty well set up for basic camping. These three items represent an investment of around $200 to $400, with the tent and sleeping bag costing about the same, while the mattress is considerably less. They represent a total of about 15 pounds of your load, especially if you have settled for one of the cheaper, synthetic-filled sleeping bags. Travel costs have already been drastically reduced by these three items of camping equipment, and they will more than pay for themselves in a very short time.

For the solo rider who wants to keep cooking chores to a minimum, I can recommend my lightest outfit. It consists of a lightweight backpacker aluminum teakettle or pot with a lid, a tiny one-burner stove, a cup, a large bowl (mine's an oval-shaped plastic vegetable dish) and a spoon. It's amazing how many different meals can be prepared with this combination. Admittedly, one must rely rather heavily on instant foods, but by just being able to boil water you can live quite comfortably. You can now fix hot drinks, soups, noodle dishes and even eggs. Add these to all the foods that don't require cooking, such as salads, fresh fruits, cold cuts and cheese, and you can really eat well. All you need for cleaning up is a small bottle of detergent, a sponge scrubber and a dish towel.

Anyone who wants to be a little more adventurous in their meal preparations should add another pot, frying pan, plate, knife and fork to the above kit. This considerably extends your range of cooking and is more than sufficient unless you are really addicted to gourmet meals.

Cooking utensils quickly add up in weight and bulk, so it pays to keep your requirements simple. No doubt you will want to add basics like salt and pepper, a cooking spoon and knife, but try to forget fancy ingredients until you get back home.

If you do any cooking over a campfire, rather than a stove, you will want to make a cloth sack for the pots and pans; otherwise, the fire-blackened pots will smudge everything in your saddlebags.

There are a great many small stoves on the market using a number of different types of fuel. Most popular are the types that use white gas, butane or kerosene. Each type has its advantages and disadvantages.

Butane stoves are the most convenient to use and the simplest to get started. However, the fuel is relatively expensive and can be quite difficult to find in the stores. All the small butane backpacker stoves use non-refillable fuel containers and the different brands are not interchangeable. This means that on long tours several fuel cartridges should be carried to avoid tedious shopping expeditions when fuel gets low. The heat output from butane stoves is lower than from the other two.

Kerosene will need priming and is really quite tedious to get started, as well as being rather dirty and smelly (although deodorized kerosene is now available). It is also inclined to leave a greasy, sooty coating on pots and pans.

This leaves white gas, which I tend to favor mainly because it is so readily available in this country. You can buy white or stove gas, usually Coleman fuel, at many sporting goods stores, hardware stores, service stations and almost anywhere that camping supplies are sold. In addition, if you run really short of fuel, unleaded pump gas can be used, although it's not to be recommended unless you are desperate. White gas stoves also need to be primed but are simpler to start than the ones using kerosene.

Most small stoves weigh between one and two pounds empty, but some hold more fuel than others so the total weight will vary accordingly, as will the amount of burning time they offer.

The type of fuel used will govern maximum temperatures available, although some white gas stoves use a pressurizing pump to obtain a substantially higher range of temperatures. It can cut your cooking time by almost half but, of course, you will use a lot more fuel and this type of stove is noticeably louder in operation.

Prices of white gas or kerosene stoves start at around $25 and can cost as much as $75. Butane models are much cheaper initially, at around $20, but the higher cost of the fuel quickly offsets any savings you have made.

After selecting your stove, you might like to consider some of the accessories that are available. If you have chosen a white gas or kerosene model, an extra fuel bottle or flask, plus a fuel funnel, can be useful. Another valuable extra is a wind shield, although it is not always easy to find something suitable. The best I have come across is an aluminum "splatter shield" available in dime stores or other places that stock inexpensive kitchen accessories.

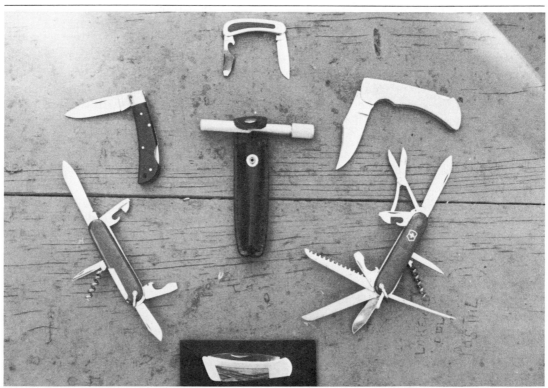

While the Swiss army style knife offers the most versatility for the camping rider, it is far from being the only knife that is appro-priate for motorcycle camping. The lock-back folding knives are both popular and practical.

Your cooking set need not be too elaborate. All you need for the one-burner stove or campfire cooking is an aluminum pan or two (sometimes called billies) and a frying pan (Teflon-lined pans are the easiest to clean), plus a kettle. As I said earlier, the kettle is one of the most useful items in my own cooking kit. It is a little hard to find, but if you shop around, you will be able to buy one of the flat, easy-to-pack, one-quart sizes.

Each person needs a set of utensils, a cup and a plate. A small spatula and a Swiss army-style knife, preferably one with a can and bottle opener attachment, should be adequate for most of your kitchen needs. Some sort of water container will be needed in most campsites, and there are a number of folding or collapsible water bottles available. One I have used for some time now was originally designed to freeze water in for use in an ice chest. It folds quite small, yet holds two quarts and pours easily. I fill it only when I have pulled into camp for the night, unlike the small water bottle I carry in the tank bag or fairing, which I keep filled all the time.

One of my favorite things about camping is the open fire and I always build one when I can. Most of the time you can easily gather your wood, if you cannot buy it, but if you are really determined to cut your own, carry a saw with you rather than an axe. One of the little folding aluminum camp saws will weigh only slightly over a pound and will cut all the firewood you need. Just be sure it is legal to cut wood where you are and stick to felled or dead trees.

Before you venture off on a major trip, you may want to take a few weekend outings fairly close to home to try out all your new equipment. This will give you an opportunity to iron out any problems and find out if there is anything extra you need. However, be careful not to add things unless they are absolutely essential.

Backpackers rely heavily on freeze-dried foods, but they are not really necessary for the touring rider, apart from perhaps tucking one or two meals away for emergency use. It is almost always possible and preferable to shop daily. I generally set up camp first and then make a food run to the nearest store, unless I plan to camp off the beaten path, in which case I will stop and shop shortly before looking for a campsite. This allows you to add plenty of fresh food to your diet and, if you are only planning to stay overnight, you need only buy enough for dinner and breakfast the following morning. For longer stops, you may wish you had some form of refrigeration and the answer could be one of the small, soft, folding ice chests that are now on the market and work well for short-term use. They can be carried folded up and filled with ice once you get into camp; they also make a good place for storing your ice-cold beer!

Each rider will make his or her own choice of equipment depending upon personal preferences, requirements and individual budgets, but at the end of it all, the total weight should fall within certain limits. The following chart will act as a guide to anyone buying new camping gear. Obviously, the lighter the weight, the better; but providing you stay within the amounts shown, you will still have room for the other things you want to take with you.

From this, we can see why two-up riders have more problems with weight and bulk; they have the most gear to pack and the least amount of space to load it.

Much of the camping equipment suggested in this chapter has been designed orig-

	Solo	Two-up
Tent	3 - 6 lbs.	5 - 10 lbs.
Sleeping bag	4 - 6 lbs.	8 - 12 lbs.
Mattress	1 - 2 lbs.	2 - 4 lbs.
Galley (including stove)	3 - 10 lbs.	5 - 12 lbs.
Totals	11 - 24 lbs.	20 - 38 lbs.

inally for the backpacker and it can be difficult, especially in smaller towns, to find a supplier. As mentioned earlier, we have helped would-be buyers by including a list of catalog sales outlets for backpacking and other camping equipment. These catalogs are a convenient way to study and compare prices and styles of equipment available. Many are full of useful advice and information that will interest anyone who really wants to get the best out of their camping.

Catalogs

Company Name and Address	Type Equipment Carried
Eddie Bauer Fifth & Union Seattle, Washington 98124	Down clothing and sleeping bags; some camping gear
LLBean Freeport, Maine 04033	Full line of equipment and clothing
Camp 7 802 South Sherman Street Longmont, Colorado 80501	Down sleeping bags and clothing
Camp Trails Company 4111 W. Clarendon Avenue Phoenix, Arizona 85019	Sleeping bags and backpacks
Early Winters 110 Prefontaine Place South Seattle, Washington 98104	Good line of tents and backpacking equipment
Eastern Mountain Sports, Inc. Vose Farm Road Peterborough, New Hampshire 03458	Full line of equipment and clothing
Lands End Yacht Stores, Inc. 2317 N. Elston Ave. Chicago, Illinois 60614	Soft luggage and clothing; excellent rainsuits

The North Face P.O. Box 2399 Station A Berkeley, California 94702	Clothing, backpacks, full line of tents and sleeping bags
Orvis Manchester, Vermont 05254	Mostly fishing tackle, but some clothing and equipment
Recreational Equipment, Inc. P.O. Box C-88125 Seattle, Washington 98188	Excellent choice of all backpacking and camping gear; good range of prices
Sierra Designs 247 Fourth Street Oakland, California 94607	Tents, clothing and sleeping bags
The Ski Hut P.O. Box 309 Berkeley, California 94701	Clothing and camping equipment
Wilderness Experience 20120 Plummer Street Chatsworth, California 91311	Backpacks, soft luggage, sleeping bags and tents

Chapter 9
Loading the Bike

Preparations for your first motorcycle tour are well underway. You have selected your bike, bought all the camping gear you'll need and have sorted out your riding clothes, casual clothes, cameras and perhaps a dab of fishing tackle. In fact, you cannot think of anything you have forgotten.

There is just one problem, though. It is all piled up in one corner of the room, and there suddenly seems to be an awful lot of gear, even though you've been really strict with yourself and rejected almost everything that was not absolutely essential.

Packing it all seems a formidable task, but you have a big set of saddlebags, a huge duffle bag and the biggest tank bag you could find, plus some space in the frame-mounted fairing. Somehow or other it must all go in.

Your problems are not over yet. You have still to weigh it all and load it onto the motorcycle, and this is where the unpacking and repacking starts. Suddenly all those instructions about careful selection and buying lightweight equipment begin to take on real significance; now you have to consider not only where to put everything, but also how much it weighs. If you start cheating here, you will end up with an overloaded machine that is, at the very least, a threat to your riding enjoyment.

Two-up riders with camping gear face the biggest loading problems and will almost always carry too much, but even the solo rider who intends to stay in motels would be well advised to keep a close check on the total weight and its distribution on the bike.

But why all this concern with weight and overloading? Does it really matter if you carry too much?

The answer is a resounding *yes*. If you ignore weight, it is all too easy to pile too much onto your bike, and the results of severe overloading can be extremely serious. It often shows up only in an emergency situation; you try to stop quickly and find it impossible, or you hit a tight corner a little too fast and find the bike will not handle. We will look more closely at the dangers of gross overloading later in the chapter, but first, what constitutes overloading?

We touched on the subject of GVWR (gross vehicle weight rating) in Chapter 3 when discussing how to select a bike for touring. Hopefully, your choice of bike offers you nearly enough the load capacity you need, but in any case, you must now live within the machine's limitations.

First, you should know exactly what the load capacity is for your bike, and for this you need to have some fairly accurate measurements. Most bikes sold since 1972 will have a plate or sticker on the steering head that lists the GVWR and the GAWR (gross axle weight rating) for both the front and rear. The figure given for the GVWR is the maximum amount that the bike should weigh completely loaded up with accessories, luggage, rider and passenger.

If your bike was built before 1972, or if it is one of the Italian models that waited until 1977 to conform to the 1972 law requiring GVWR plates, you can get a rough idea of the GVWR from the figures given on the tires. Each tire on a bike is required by the Department of Transportation to indicate its maximum weight-carrying capacity. This figure appears on the side wall close to the rim and will read something like "max load 690 pounds @ 40 psi cold."

The figure given on the rear tire is the most useful, since it will be very close to the maximum weight allowance for the rear axle. The weight recommended on the front tire, however, is likely to be higher than the amount of weight you would want to carry on the front of a motorcycle.

You will have difficulty working out the GVWR if the manufacturer does not provide it. As a fairly rough guide, you can take the figure given on the rear tire and add it to 70% of the figure given on the front. The only alternative is to try to locate a bike the same make and model as yours but of more recent manufacture and trust that the GVWR will be nearly the same.

A few years ago I had the opportunity to discuss bike-loading capacities with design engineers from most of the major motorcycle manufacturers. They all agreed that while GVWR takes into account such things as frame strength and rigidity, brakes and suspension, by far the major limiting factor is the tires. This means that the figure given for maximum load capacity on the rear tire must be strictly observed to keep from overloading the bike.

Before doing any further calculations, you will need to know exactly how much the bike weighs without its load. It can be difficult to find suitable scales, but you will only need to do it once, so it is worth going to a bit of trouble to get accurate figures.

Ideally, you want to use a stationary scale—one mounted flush to the floor with at least a 1,000-pound range. Sometimes companies dealing with moving freight will have this type of scale. You might also try junkyards or produce packing and shipping companies. As a last resort, you could use commercial truck scales, but since these only weigh in 20-pound increments you will not be able to get a very accurate figure.

Take three weights: the weight of the entire bike, its front end only and rear only. Make sure the fuel tank is almost full and leave on any bolted-on accessories, plus things like the tool kit which are always kept on the bike. The fairing and saddlebags should be empty since you will be weighing the luggage separately.

Once you have these three figures, record them in the bike's logbook or wherever they will be safe and easily accessible. These will be the basis of all your loading calculations and they will only change if you alter your bike's accessories.

From now on, you will be able to manage with a good bathroom scale. Incidentally, you will get a more accurate result if you step on the scale yourself, holding the articles to be weighed and then subtract your own weight. This way the scale is operating in the middle range, which is the most accurate.

For your final calculations you will also need to know the weight of rider and regular passenger, both fully dressed for riding complete with helmets. The rider's weight will be distributed 25% to the front and 75% to the rear, for the sake of your calculations, whereas the passenger's weight only affects the rear wheel.

This completes your basic weight data, which will vary only slightly from trip to trip. The main variables will be the amount of luggage you take with you. If you find you need to take extra, you can always consider putting your passenger on a diet!

Let us now look at a working example in order to get a better idea of the reason for these calculations and to provide some useful guidelines. We will take an 1100cc machine that weighs 612 pounds and has a GVWR of 1,090 pounds, giving an initial load capacity of 478 pounds. By adding a frame-mounted fairing with lowers, we use up 42 pounds (including the mounting equipment); a set of saddlebags plus mounts and a luggage rack add another 37 pounds. This brings the basic weight to 691 pounds without riders or luggage—and this is on a machine that has no engine guard bars, floor boards, extra lights, or any of the other favored accessories. However, this still leaves us a fairly respectable 399 pounds, so it looks as if we should be able to manage. Our rider is a 175-pound male, who weighs 190 pounds in his riding gear. If he travels alone, he will have 209 pounds available for load, which should be more than enough.

This becomes drastically reduced, however, if he has a 150-pound passenger. Now their combined luggage must weigh just 59 pounds, and suddenly all the talk about lightweight this and lightweight that starts to make sense. It is obvious that the touring couple will be unable to avoid overloading their machine unless the bike is virtually stripped of accessories and they carry the minimum of luggage; there is certainly little chance of carrying camping equipment and staying within the recommended load limit. Now every pound of weight becomes not just a pound of load, but a pound of *overload*, making each one far more important.

The situation looks rather bleak, but there is no need to give up on the idea of two-up touring. Your machine does not suddenly become unsafe just because you are a few pounds overloaded; the maximum load indicated by the manufacturer is simply a recommended limit, after which the bike's performance may be affected.

Rear suspension is usually the first thing to suffer when a bike is heavily loaded, since the steel springs used on most motorcycles do not offer the latitude needed for both solo riding and two-up touring. Any large load, even one within the GVWR, is likely to cause the machine to bottom out over bad road surfaces. Fortunately, there are several ways to improve the bike's suspension and, if you are planning to do most of your miles two-up and loaded, heavy-duty steel springs may offer an inexpensive and reliable remedy. Air springs at the rear offer greater flexibility and are being fitted as standard equipment on more and more new machines. If your bike does not already have them, they would be well worth considering if you wish to be able to switch easily from solo riding to two-up touring.

Any improvement in the rear suspension will help the bike's overall handling ability, especially its straight-line stability. Obviously, we are not looking for road-racer potential from a big, heavily loaded touring machine, but it is important that it should feel comfortable when ridden sensibly. You will quickly tire if you are having to struggle with your bike every inch of the way.

There is one other adjustment that must be made if you are close to, or over, the maximum weight rating. The air pressure in the rear tire needs to be increased to its maximum, which is listed on the tire's sidewall and will vary depending on whether it was manufactured to U.S., Japanese or European standards. The added air pressure will make the ride a little harder, but it should make it easier to negotiate curves at reasonable speeds.

Adjustment to your bike's suspension and the correct air pressure will improve the way the bike feels—in some cases dramatically. It is important that you do not allow it to induce a false sense of security. Your bike is still overloaded and you must be aware of it at all times so that you can compensate with the necessary adjustments to your riding style, speed, following distances and so on.

Even a grossly overloaded bike can be ridden, providing the weight is well distributed and that the rider takes extra care. Indeed, Continental Tires states in its catalog that if the rider keeps speeds down he can greatly increase his load. For example, for tires rated at 130 mph, the maximum load rating can be increased by up to 25% if speeds are kept below 60 mph. This would mean that the 670-pound maximum rating for a 4.50 x 17 tire would be increased to 837.5 pounds if this speed restriction was observed—a healthy difference of 167.5 pounds in load capacity.

Braking is another important feature likely to be seriously affected by overloading. Unfortunately, you may not realize the full extent to which it has been impaired until you need to stop in an emergency. If you really need convincing, take your unloaded bike out on the road and measure braking distances from different speeds. Try it again with your bike fully loaded for touring, complete with passenger if possible, and note the difference. It feels like another motorcycle, doesn't it? In effect, it *is* since it now has completely different braking and handling characteristics of which you should be aware.

Every effort must obviously be made to keep overall weight within the manufacturer's limits, but it is reassuring to know that all is not lost if this proves an impossible task. If you make the necessary adjustments to your motorcycle and modify your riding style, you should still be able to tour in comfort and safety.

However, overall weight is not the whole story. Distribution of the load also plays a big part in the effect on the motorcycle. In general, it is best to keep the weight as near the center of gravity as possible, both fore and aft, and evenly balanced side to side.

Suppose we place the bike's center of gravity directly under the rider's footpegs

When loading a bike, bulk of the weight should be in Zone A, with lightweight items in Zones B.

and draw two lines vertically through the bike, one at the steering head and the other through the rear axle. We can see that these two lines bind an almost equal area on both sides of the center of gravity. It is also fairly clear from the illustration that the rider and passenger fall within these two lines.

To help in identification, we will call the area between the lines area A and the area outside the lines area B. Obviously, area A is by far the more preferable place to carry weight, but unfortunately there are only a limited number of storage places available. Perhaps the most convenient spot is on top of the fuel tank, making the tank bag one of the most desirable pieces of touring luggage. You will rarely see an experienced touring rider without one. The tank bag sits almost on top of the center of

An example of how not
*to load a bike. Overloading and
poor pre-planning will almost assure
troubles on the road.*

gravity so it will have little effect on the bike's handling, and its weight will have only a mild effect on braking distances.

The second-best location is the front section of the saddlebags, especially the area that falls in front of the rear axle. Saddlebags have the added attraction of distributing weight relatively low on the bike—very desirable since this has little effect on handling around curves and adds to straight-line stability in crosswinds.

About the only other conventional place for storage that falls into area A is the section nearest to the rider in the pockets of a frame-mounted fairing.

If, however, a large fairing is not used, it would be possible to have some soft, throw-over saddlebags resting on either side of the fuel tank. These seem to have gone out of fashion lately, but if you can keep them away from the engine and out of your way, they can offer a fair amount of well-located storage space.

One spot within area A often ignored is carrying space on the rider and passenger, in the pockets of jackets, shirts and pants. There is also the belt where a knife, either folding or Swiss-army style, can be carried. Nylon backpacker belt pouches also prove very useful for carrying valuables, such as a small camera, logbook, address and phone books, checkbook and money.

There seems to be a reasonable amount of usable space within area A, but it does have its limitations in both size and volume of things that can be carried. Long items present a real packing problem since most saddlebags will not take anything over 18 or 20 inches, and fairing pockets and tank bags are even more restrictive. Anything between 20 and 36 inches usually ends up being packed across the luggage rack. It is possible to carry longer items, but they can present a problem since the width of a big touring bike is rarely more than three feet.

I once had a two-piece fishing rod that I desperately wanted to take with me on a long trip, but in its shortest form it was 50 inches. I eventually found a spot for it just below the level of the fuel tank, alongside the engine cases, extending back under the edge of the seat. I had a vinyl case custom made to fit with tie straps where they were needed. That rod accompanied me on many subsequent trips and survived all sorts of mishaps without damage. While this example may be slightly unusual, it does show that almost anything essential can be packed on a motorcycle if you are prepared to put some thought into it.

Storage space available in area B needs to be used, but it is worth keeping in mind the reasons why it is less desirable.

Perhaps surprisingly, one of the worst places to carry anything much is the luggage rack—surprising since you would imagine anything designed as carrying space would be ideally suited to the purpose. It is quite a good place to load light, larger items, but it is thoroughly inadvisable to use it for anything heavy since it places the weight high and some distance behind the rear axle. This results in its exerting more influence on the bike's handling than its carrying capacity justifies.

One riding friend told me about a small wobble that had developed in the front end of his machine at certain speeds. It was nothing serious, just annoying. He tried to cure it by buying new tires, replacing the head bearing, as well as checking and realigning everything he thought could have caused the problem, but with no success. Eventually, he mentioned it to his dealer while his bike was in for minor servicing. He was told to try removing the small "sissy bar" from the back of the seat. Doubting that it would work but willing to try anything, my friend removed the bar and, sure enough, it cured the problem.

I have had similar experiences with travel trunks and heavy loads on luggage racks which invariably show up on the front of the bike and can be quite nasty if not detected in time. For this reason, I try to reserve the luggage rack for long, light, bulky items such as tents, sleeping bags and mats. If you are riding solo, it is much better to use the passenger seat for these items and leave the luggage rack empty.

Every now and then I have seen bikes with a sleeping bag or some other short item lashed on to the front fender. This is a very foolish practice and I would not recommend it at any time. Most bike manufacturers go to great lengths to reduce unsprung weight, so to add weight to the front fender defeats all their efforts to produce a bike that handles well.

It is a potentially dangerous practice since anything carried here could get in the way of braking, steering or even prevent the front wheel from rolling freely. It is also likely to cause engine damage by obstructing the free flow of air which is the engine's only cooling system on the majority of bikes. The idea of getting some of the weight forward is a good one, but settle for a tank bag—it is a far safer solution.

It is a good idea to keep everything on your bike loaded into a bag, be it a tank bag, duffle bag or saddlebag. Not only does this help to keep your luggage clean and dry, but it also makes loading and unloading much simpler, and it is good security against getting your equipment stolen. A nondescript duffle bag looks infinitely less desirable than a smart-looking down sleeping bag, or your favorite leather jacket.

Most frame-mounted fairings offer a good amount of useful storage space, but here also, weight distribution is important. It is best to place heavy items in the area just in front of the rider's knees and, since it is a convenient place to get into at fuel stops and so on, it makes a good place to keep your chain lube, air pressure and tread depth gauges, as well as waterproof gloves, boots and mitts.

Rainsuits can also be kept in the fairing since it keeps them accessible, even if it is sometimes a little awkward to extract them from the pockets. It is also a good place for your down or electric vest.

I have already praised the tank bag for its ideal location, but it is worth a second mention since it is such a convenient and safe place to keep important items. Many are designed to unclip easily from a base attached to the fuel tank, so they can easily be removed if you need to fill up with gas and, even more important, can be taken with you whenever you are out of sight of the bike. This makes a tank bag ideal for your valuable items, such as cameras, binoculars and traveler's checks, especially as it is in view the whole time you are traveling. In addition, it is easy to get into, so it makes a good place for regularly used items such as your suntan lotion, motorcycle logbook, and water bottle. Many tank bags have a transparent cover on the top, which makes an ideal spot for your map, route plan or travel literature as, no doubt, it was designed to be. Since the oil companies started charging for maps, I have found it makes sense to leave home with any I think might be needed on the trip.

Generally, I use the front of the saddlebags for heavy camping items such as the galley gear, which includes the stove and spare fuel, if the latter has not already found its way into the tank bag or fairing pocket. The rest of the space is then available for clothing.

As previously mentioned, the luggage rack makes a good place for the tent, sleeping bags and foam mats, as well as for riding suits if they will not fit elsewhere. All of these items are best kept together in a duffle bag. Alternatively, the sleeping bags can be secured on top of the saddlebags, which can prove especially valuable for the touring couple short of space. There are a number of ways to fasten items to the saddlebags, but I have found one of the most satisfactory to be using the little chromed hooks, or eyes for that matter, sold at marine stores. These need to be screwed to the saddlebag and bungee straps can then be used to fasten the items down.

There are several other places on the bike that can be used for storage if you only know about them. One of these is underneath the luggage rack where I have often carried a bike cover, as well as rainsuits if I have been almost certain they will not be needed urgently. Most bikes will have a few useful spots for packing away extra items and almost all machines will have enough room in the headlight and taillight for stowing spare bulbs and fuses, if they are not already fitted elsewhere.

Learning to use every nook and cranny is particularly important for the two-up riders who are faced with the demanding task of first cutting their load down to a reasonable size and weight, and then trying to fit everything onto the bike in some semblance of order.

Whether solo or two-up, it makes sense to pack everything into as small a space as possible and, to achieve this, I rely on a good supply of rubber bands. The old army trick of rolling clothing for packing works well on socks and underwear, but almost any clothing can be rolled if you secure it with rubber bands. Even western shirts can be packed this way, rolled from the tail so that the collar is on the outside to stay in better shape. You will probably need large rubber bands to stretch around rolled riding clothes, but it is easy enough to find old inner tubes from which you can cut bands of just the width you need. Bicycle inner tubes, motorcycle inner tubes and, finally, car inner tubes will provide almost all the rubber bands you need, but if extra large ones are required, you can use truck inner tubes. Rainsuits, rubber overboots and riding suits will all be reduced in size if they are rolled and secured by rubber bands, which brings me to one final point.

When loading the bike, be sure to pack, or leave space for, *all* riding clothes, except items that are sure to be worn at all times. I well remember one trip when my passenger and I packed the bike up late one night to be ready for an early start and, knowing the morning would be cool, left out all our warm riding gear. As usual, every last remaining space was filled with essentials, and we felt quite pleased that we had finally managed to find a place for everything.

However, 250 miles out the following day, we found we did not need our heavy riding suits any longer. And, guess what! There was no place left on the bike for them. Eventually, I found a suitable place, but the whole trip was difficult because we were fighting for space.

Try not to fill every last inch before you leave home since you never know when you might need one more place for something and, if you are planning to wear layers of clothes when you set out, be sure there is space left to store them when the sun shines!

Chapter 10
Trailers and Sidecars

Trailers may not add much excitement to your riding experience, but they can solve the problem of carrying unwieldy items when touring. Trailers are definitely worth considering in certain circumstances, but only if you are prepared to make the necessary adjustments to your riding technique. This highlights the need to decide exactly what you want from touring. If the riding itself is the main attraction and you wish to experience the thrill of riding at road speed on winding, twisting roads, then you should not even consider towing a trailer. On the other hand, if you are expecting to enjoy long quiet periods in camp, with time to go hiking, fishing or even boating, then a trailer might be a worthwhile addition to your touring setup.

Throughout this book, we have constantly stressed the need to keep weight down; to take less, so the bike is more fun to ride. Trailers are for anyone who does not wish to practice the self-discipline and restraint that doing-with-less requires. Some riders may feel there are certain items that they simply must take. These can be just personal "bits and pieces" without which a vacation is not a vacation, or items essential to work or play. This was true in the case of one Canadian couple, Paul and Lauren Goulet, who decided to take an extended honeymoon and tour on a motorcycle for a year. Since they could not afford a year-long sabbatical, they had to spend part of the time working, which meant the addition of heavy tools for Paul and extra work clothes for both of them. They intended to camp most of the year, so they needed a few extra nonessential items that would make life a little more comfortable. Realizing they couldn't expect a single motorcycle to cope with everything they wanted to take, they decided to tow a small clamshell-style trailer.

The trailer was fairly light, made of fiberglass, and it looked a bit like two bathtubs, one upside down on top of the other and hinged on one side. The floor was designed to make into a good-sized, fairly comfortable bed, which eliminated the need for a separate tent. The only problem was that the whole trailer had to be unloaded before the bed could be used. While traveling, there was ample space to store extra gear on top of the bed and this led to a terrible temptation to take far too much luggage. "If you think it's difficult to say no when you only have two saddlebags, you should try doing it with that huge empty space in the trailer looking at you," Paul told me. He admitted they'd started out with too much gear, taking boxes, bags and suitcases full of "just in case" items that in retrospect they realized they could have done without. Since they were going to be gone a full year, it was all too easy to get caught up in the "it might be nice to have" syndrome.

Anyone who has never used a trailer may be wondering about all this fuss over weight, since the load is not actually on the bike. This is a valid point, but the fact remains that weight in the trailer can have a considerable effect on the motorcycle. Indeed, the greater the trailer weight, the greater the effect on the bike's overall performance. At least 10% of the total weight should be on the hitch, and hence on the bike, but this is something we will discuss later in the chapter.

First, let us look more closely at some of the advantages and disadvantages of trailers. As already mentioned, the greatest benefit is the ability to carry a considerable amount of equipment—far more than you would ever dream of loading onto a motorcycle. Trailers provide a reasonable solution for riders who take their camping seriously and who want to carry a lot of equipment. These riders might consider not only the standard utility models designed to carry any type of heavy equipment, but also the tent trailers, designed specifically with the camper in mind.

Utility trailers have a wide range of uses and will suit anyone who likes to follow other pursuits while on motorcycling vacations. I met a couple fishing in Minnesota who pulled a small utility trailer behind their bike to carry a high quality, inflatable boat, a 10hp outboard motor, fishing tackle and all their camping gear. They would select a campsite near a lake, set up a base camp and then intersperse days of fishing with day trips on the bike.

Surprisingly, a loaded trailer can sometimes, just *sometimes,* offer increased stability to the motorcycle. On occasions when it is essential to keep the bike from veering, the trailer can provide enough drag to make it possible. One incident that comes to mind occurred when I was towing a trailer from Phoenix, Arizona, back to Los Angeles. It was a fair-sized trailer, with about a 200-pound load, and I made the mistake of pulling off the road onto what looked like a solid shoulder but turned out to be soft sand. I was traveling a bit fast, since there was a car close behind, and the sand seemed too soft to safely apply the brakes. However, thanks to the drag of the trailer, it was possible to just coast to a stop. When I pulled back out of the sand, the trailer was again an asset in helping keep the bike stable. Later, on the same trip, I again had occasion to be thankful for the added stability provided by the trailer. This time I was riding through an extremely heavy desert thunderstorm which left streams of water several inches deep on parts of the road. With the help of the trailer, I could hit these patches of water at around 50 mph and still keep the bike from swerving.

A riding friend told me he'd experienced much the same thing in a heavy snowstorm between Laramie and Cheyenne, Wyoming. "The snow was slushy, even though it was four or five inches deep in places and I could feel the bike slipping some. I kept the speed around 20 mph and the trailer kept me going straight. I'm not sure I would have made it without that trailer," he said. Unfortunately, it is only on rare occasions such

Adding the length and weight of a trailer not only changes the bike's appearance, but calls for a decidedly more conservative riding style. It's best to get in some practice in handling the trailer before hitting the open road.

as these that the trailer is actually a help. Far more often it proves to be detrimental to the motorcycle's performance.

Most severely affected, in most everyday situations, are braking distances. It's all too easy to forget about the weight of a trailer, particularly with a large capacity motorcycle which should have enough power to cope with the extra load. Certainly, a properly loaded trailer should cause few problems when you're traveling on a straight course and there seems little need to alter normal riding styles. However, it is essential to remember that braking will be affected. I am not aware that any of the trailers

designed for motorcycles are equipped with brakes. You are entirely dependent upon the bike's braking system to do the job. Normally, the rider will automatically use a little more brake and, nine times out of ten, this works adequately. That tenth occasion is the one you should be conscious of at all times. The serious reduction in emergency braking capability is the biggest problem of towing a trailer behind a motorcycle. Part of the problem is caused by the added weight, but in braking tests I have found that it is more than just weight. The trailer hitch acts as a hinge and under heavy braking the trailer tends to push the rear of the bike around, greatly adding to your stopping difficulties. There is a massive weight transfer to the front of a motorcycle under heavy braking, with or without a trailer, which can be observed in the compression of the front suspension. This explains in part why the front brake does so much of the work in stopping the bike. As the weight on the front increases, there is a corresponding decrease in weight at the rear. This weight transfer becomes even more exaggerated when a trailer is being towed, which makes it frighteningly easy to lock the rear wheel.

It is bad enough having to cope with a locked back wheel on a loaded motorcycle,

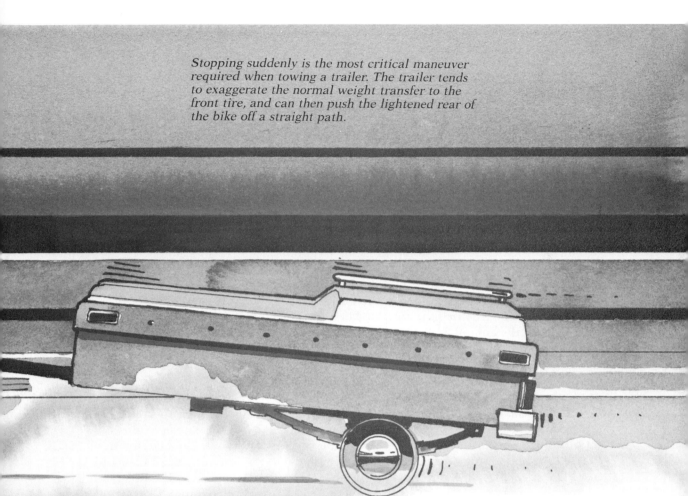

Stopping suddenly is the most critical maneuver required when towing a trailer. The trailer tends to exaggerate the normal weight transfer to the front tire, and can then push the lightened rear of the bike off a straight path.

but with a trailer in tow it becomes a potential disaster. We now have the inertia of several hundred pounds of trailer, without brakes, pushing on a point 1½ feet behind the rear tire; the rear of the bike has, in effect, grown lighter under such heavy braking and, as it raises on the suspension, it lifts the hitch point. This makes jackknifing a very real danger. I had my worst fears about stopping a trailer confirmed by a rider in Colorado, whom I first noticed because he was on crutches, being helped to his bike by a friend. The injured rider was on a Gold Wing with fairing, saddlebags, travel trunk and trailer. I learned that he had injured his leg a couple of days earlier in a road accident. Apparently he had been following a car through a small town and had failed to make allowances for the trailer he was towing. When the car braked suddenly, he realized as soon as he started braking that he was too close to stop and had to veer off the road to avoid the car, ending up in a ditch. This rider had plenty of experience with the bike/trailer combination and was well aware of stopping distances, but as he said, "I forgot, was in a bit of a hurry and got caught!" Luckily the bike damage was minimal, but he admitted, "Yeah, I probably could have stopped in time without the trailer."

Normally, he said he would have doubled or even trebled his following distances when towing the trailer, but on this occasion his mind had been elsewhere and he'd momentarily forgotten the trailer was there.

Braking aside, the adverse effects of a trailer are surprisingly few. A trailer will require more room when turning and the extra width must be taken into account, but the motorcycle will still lean normally, and most of the time the trailer will be barely noticeable. The same cannot be said of sidecars. While they are functionally similar to trailers, in that they can both be used to carry extra gear, this is about all they have in common. Sidecars are comparatively expensive and effect much greater changes in appearance and riding style. You will be constantly aware of a sidecar and, in most outfits, the bike no longer leans. With a right-hand-mounted chair, the bike will pull to the right under acceleration and to the left under deceleration. Some riders become extremely proficient at sidecar riding, but it does require practice and normal motorcycle training is not sufficient. Sidecars offer a number of unique benefits and undoubtedly the major advantage is their ability to carry extra passengers. It is possible for a family of three or four to tour fairly comfortably in a sidecar rig and, indeed, many do. At the annual Griffith Park sidecar gathering in Los Angeles, there were outfits consisting of bike, sidecar *and* trailer. With this sort of setup, camping can be positively luxurious, allowing for big tents, lawn furniture, ice chests and stoves—with room left over for children and pets. It is a different style of motorcycle touring, but one that undoubtedly suits some riders.

If you decide a trailer is the answer for you, there are a few important factors to keep in mind before you rush out and buy one. First and foremost, you should pay attention to the trailer's weight. Most motorcycle trailers are far heavier than they need to be and all too often they are simply small car trailers converted for motorcycle use. The suspension system must be suitable for the loads you intend to carry, but bear in mind that there is a strict limit even on these loads. I have found 200 pounds to be a workable maximum weight for trailer plus load. Obviously, the lighter the trailer the more load you can carry. This indicates a small utility trailer and a fairly limited load that will, however, provide considerably more load capacity than the 30- to 50-pound limit imposed on most trailer-less motorcycle touring riders.

Overall trailer size is important, too. Most large capacity touring machines are about 36 inches wide, with or without accessories, so this is a workable trailer width. Most trailers are about this size, or slightly wider. Until the rider gets used to towing, there is always the risk of bumping into the curb or sliding off the edge of the road, so it is probably a good idea for the inexperienced trailerist to stick to one of the narrower models. Trailer length is less critical than width, although big differences in wheelbase length are noticeable. Wheelbase on a trailer is the distance between the hitch and the axle and the longer wheelbase is usually more desirable. Trailers with long wheelbases are less likely to sway violently when exposed to strong winds or poor road surfaces; their's is a more gentle rocking motion which is much easier to control. Trailers with a wheelbase between 4½ and five feet are more manageable under these conditions.

There are two major trailer styles available for motorcycles. The camping models feature built-in or fold-out beds, with some form of cover that can be raised. These tend to be long; the body is normally a little over six feet, with an additional two feet for the tongue. This effectively doubles the length of the bike, but it should tow well. The long wheelbase (usually about 5½ feet) will allow it to track satisfactorily but, because of the overall length, it will be difficult to maneuver in tight situations unless you unhook it from the bike, which is often the easiest solution. Most test trailers of this size are rather heavy, ranging from around 300 pounds to a staggering 500 pounds. Few riders can resist adding a few luxuries since there is so much space, and this added weight can get grossly out of hand from a safety standpoint. If this degree of camping luxury is an absolute must for you, I would suggest you seriously consider towing your trailer with some vehicle other than a motorcycle. There is no denying that high weights are regularly towed by motorcycles, but it places considerable constraints on the rider, who must be constantly aware of the extreme braking problems.

There are several different types of hitches available. Manufacturers are always coming up with some marvelous new "universal" hitch, but from my experience, the plain old ball style works as well as any, even though it is a little heavy. About the only precaution necessary is to ensure adequate side-to-side movement so the bike can lean while the trailer stays on an even keel. Mounting the hitch is generally a custom welding job, due to the relatively few sales of motorcycle trailers and the difficulties of making hitches to fit all bikes. It seems to work best if the hitch is attached to sprung parts of

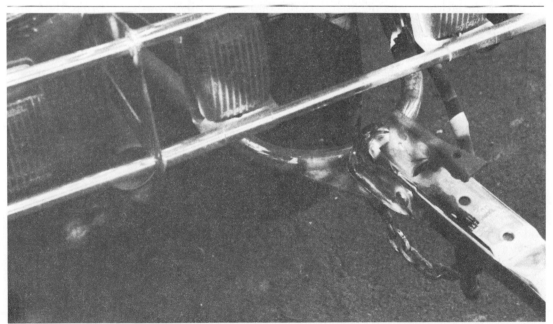

The conventional ball style hitch is simple, relatively inexpensive, and works well with a bike and trailer combination.

the bike, as opposed to unsprung parts such as swing arms or axle. The top shock mount is a popular choice, with the passenger footpegs a good second attachment point. Both are considerably better than one hitching arrangement I saw where a rider had completely eliminated his rear suspension movement by mounting a nonflexing hitch to the rear axle and top shock mount!

Hooking up the lights from bike to trailer can be a problem. Most bikes have separate circuits for the turn indicators and brake lights, so four wire hookups are necessary to cover left turn signal, right turn signal, brake lights and taillights. Unfortunately, most trailer brake/turn lights are on a common wire, as they are designed like American-made cars, which have a three-wire setup (one for left turn and brake, one for right turn and brake, and one for taillights). When selecting a trailer for motorcycle use, you can save yourself trouble by checking for separate turn indicator and brake light wires.

If, however, your trailer is designed for American-made cars, which have three wires, there are converters available to handle the wiring of bike to trailer. These converters are designed for wiring a European-made car to an American-made trailer, and work quite well in wiring a trailer to a motorcycle. The converter costs about $10 and is usually available from dealers who sell tent trailers.

Side marker lights on a trailer are a sensible idea, and these can easily be wired from the taillight circuit—but be wary of adding too many lights to your bike's system. On one installation it was necessary to disconnect the bike's taillight, brake light and rear turn indicators, when the trailer was hooked up, to prevent excessive drain on the electrical system.

When choosing your trailer, don't forget to look at the suspension. While it is not a critical factor, the proper suspension will make the trailer more pleasant to use. A light trailer with a moderate load requires only a lightweight suspension system. If the springs are big and heavy and offer virtually no deflection when the trailer is empty, it is probably not suitable for motorcycle use. A trailer with overly stiff suspension is almost as bad as a trailer with no suspension at all, as both will bounce around excessively and make bike handling difficult on poorly surfaced roads. It is important that any trailer be loaded properly and there are certain basic rules to keep in mind in this regard. Heavy items should be placed directly over the axle, evenly balanced on both sides and placed as close to the floor as possible. The idea is to keep the center of gravity as low as possible and over the axle. If the floor of the trailer is fairly spacious and smooth, it is worthwhile building low sills around the area over the axle to prevent heavy items from shifting in transit. Once the heavier items have been packed in over the axle, the lighter items can be distributed around and over them, with a little additional weight toward the hitch.

A tongue weight of 15% of the total weight works well, but anything between 10% and 20% is acceptable. It is better to err on the heavy side. Since weight is going to be an important aspect of trailer handling, it makes sense to know the exact weight that you are towing, along with the hitch weight. This enables you to work out that all-important percentage of hitch weight to total weight, as well. It is also worth keeping a trip record book in which you record comments on trailer handling at the different weights; eventually you will be able to establish your most desirable towing weight.

First you must know the weight of the empty trailer. If it is under 400 pounds you can use a bathroom scale. The weights must be recorded when the trailer is level (in normal towing attitude). To accomplish this, you'll need a board or block that is the same height as the scale, and a pile of bricks or blocks that can be used to keep the tongue at normal height. First, position a block under one wheel and the scale under the other. Use blocks to keep the tongue level. Record the wheel weight figure, and transpose the block and scale to record the other wheel weight figure.

Remove the block and scale so the tires are on the ground. Place the scale under the tongue, along with a suitable number of blocks so the tongue is level. Record the tongue weight figure.

If you then weigh each item loaded into the trailer, you can accurately calculate the weight of the loaded trailer. This should give you a good idea of the effect it will have on your motorcycle under heavy braking. You also need to determine whether hitch weight is within 10% to 20% of the total.

This may seem like a lot of fuss and bother, but it is an important task if you are going to travel safely on a motorcycle towing a trailer. In short, if you keep the load light, pack it correctly and remember to allow plenty of room for stopping, your trailer should give you no cause for concern.

Chapter 11
Selecting a Touring Area

If you enjoy maps as much as I do, trip planning becomes one of the many pleasurable aspects of touring. Selecting travel areas is one of your first—and most important—tasks, and it is not always an easy one, so to start with we are going to look at ways to make it simpler.

Many of us immediately opt for an area as far away as we think we can reach in the time available. That's fine if you just want to achieve a high-mileage trip, but to me this is motorcycle traveling and not touring. I prefer the latter if I have a choice.

Let me explain further. If you are trying to cover a lot of ground, to reach a far-distant destination in a fairly short vacation, you will be looking at high-mileage days and long hours in the saddle. It is difficult to put an exact figure on it, but we are probably talking about traveling more than 300 miles every day, which will represent at least six hours of riding. By the time we have added a couple of meal stops and some fuel stops, it pretty quickly adds up to a full day on the road. Obviously, this leaves little or no time for any sightseeing, certainly no time for browsing around museums, and no chance of making unscheduled diversions along back roads that really don't lead anywhere. That, to me, is the chief difference between motorcycle traveling and touring. I will travel on the interstate, but I would never tour on it. I consider that touring is done mainly on two-lane roads—the kind that follow the contours of the land and run through small towns and villages. It allows time for frequent breaks from riding to admire a spectacular view, or shoot some pictures, or just wander through some place that looks interesting.

So, before deciding where you are headed, consider what you want to get from your trip. If you want to be able to experience the country, rather than just have it flash by, and if you intend to meet the people, as well as learn a little about the history we share, then you will want to schedule a great many "touring" days throughout the trip. Alternatively, if you prefer to cover great distances day after day, wasting no time admiring views or absorbing the atmosphere, then that is your choice. Personally, I would think that, unless there is some all-important reason for traveling this way, you are wasting an ideal opportunity to have some unique experiences.

Unfortunately, we have grown up with the definition of travel as being a measurement of miles. It is all too common to hear riders boast that "it only took us two days to travel 1,800 miles," and no one ever thinks to ask whether they learned, or even saw, anything. Chances are they did not. Many of us need to teach ourselves to tour. We need to carefully consider the time available for our trip and plan accordingly. Obviously, it does not make sense to pick an area 1,000 miles away if all we have is a long weekend. On the other hand, few of us would be satisfied to spend a two-week vacation touring within 500 miles of home, even though there is nothing much wrong with that. What is really needed is some kind of time-distance formula that will give us some indication of the areas from which we can select. It will depend on several personal factors, in particular, the maximum amount of miles you could hope to do on your machine in one day. This will depend largely on the size of your bike and its age, as well as on your own preferences and capabilities.

I regularly start off with a first-day run of about 700 miles. This means an early start (on the road between 4 and 5 a.m.) and a full day of riding. It pretty much represents my personal upper limit for one day and is probably a lot higher than the average rider, since I have the advantage of having done a great deal of long-distance riding and am almost always on motorcycles especially suited to this sort of travel. A more realistic figure for a less experienced touring rider would be about 350 miles on a high-mileage day, with perhaps a slightly higher figure for the first day on the road. Even this is dependent upon your machine being in first-rate condition mechanically and being capable of sustained high speeds on the interstate, without tiring you out. Your personal mileage figure may end up being higher or lower than this, but for the sake of our basic calculations, we will be considering a 350-mile figure as average for travel days. Of course, this also depends largely on the type of roads available, and here we are assuming that a fair proportion of the day will be spent on fast roads, such as the interstate. It would be very difficult to ride this far in one day on congested or badly surfaced roads, so this should also be taken into account.

Up until now, we have been talking in terms of complete days, i.e., travel days and touring days. Obviously, it does not have to be broken down in this manner. For instance, on a two-day trip you might devote the first few hours of riding on the first day to "travel," to get a couple of hundred miles out to the area you want to tour. Then, after a leisurely lunch, you could spend the rest of the time within a fairly confined area. It makes sense, in this case, to set up camp or find a room at around noon on the first day. You can then unload the bike and be free to ride about in the locality for the remainder of that day and much of the next, until it is time to think about heading back home.

However, this will depend largely upon your familiarity with the area and your personal preferences. If the places on the route between your home and two-day destination are unfamiliar, you may prefer to take the whole of the first day to get there, stopping often to explore and making plenty of short detours. But if you know the route well, it makes more sense to cover it as quickly as possible to allow more time for exploring new territory farther afield. Weekend outings are quite easy to plan, since there are relatively few options. One- or two-week trips are more difficult, as they offer a great many different possibilities.

One way to start your selection procedure is to take a map, pencil and piece of string and draw concentric circles on the map, each a 350-mile increment from your home. Each circle represents at least two days' travel time (there and back), unless you are not expecting to return until a later date. These are travel days, so you will need to add to them to allow for touring days. In most cases, it is reasonable to add about half the number again. For example, a 1,750-mile trip would represent 10 travel days or a 15-day touring vacation. This is obviously only a very rough guide, but it highlights a number of important considerations that should be made when planning your tour, in order that it can be enjoyed rather than just endured.

Now that we have some idea how far from home we can expect to travel, we can start selecting desirable areas. Most riders will be looking for much the same things, such as good scenery, interesting roads and perhaps a few historical sites. Most parts of the country will meet some or all of these requirements, although some areas obviously offer more than others.

Let us imagine we have a two-week vacation; this usually amounts to 14 days plus an extra weekend, a total of 16 days on the road if we want it. We have already established our personal daily travel distances and marked them off in circles on our map as described earlier. Next, we must consider what areas would be most suitable to visit, taking into account the time of year. If you already have a particular place in mind, it would be worth arranging your vacation to coincide with the best time to tour in that area. We are quite fortunate here in the United States in that, due to the varying weather conditions throughout the country, there is almost always somewhere suitable for touring.

Few riders would consider December, January or February to be good months for traveling, but it is an ideal time of the year to visit Death Valley or San Diego County's Anza Borega Desert State Park, both in Southern California, or the area around Tucson, Arizona. It is also still possible to tour in the southernmost parts of Texas and Florida.

Anywhere in the country is accessible throughout June to August, although the above-mentioned southern areas would be among the least desirable, as are the desert stretches of the Southwest. All of Canada can be enjoyed at this time of the year.

Perhaps not surprisingly, the Rocky Mountains attract a great many touring riders to both sides of the Canadian-U.S. border. This area can be especially delightful in the fall, from around the second week in September to the first week in October, but you will be at the mercy of the weather, which is notorious for its unpredictability in these mountain areas. If you are lucky with the weather, some of the higher elevations will offer great rides through magnificent scenery, with the aspen trees having turned almost golden as they prepare to shed their leaves for the winter. This special season in the high mountains moves south at a fairly rapid pace, which varies considerably from year to year. It usually starts around early September in the Jasper National Park area on the Alberta, British Colombia border in Canada. As we move farther south, the season starts later, so that in southern Colorado and northern New Mexico, it could take effect as late as the middle of October. Generally, there is about three weeks' difference between the start of the season in the far north and its arrival in the far south.

It can be well worthwhile taking a chance on the weather, since the rewards are so many. Riding can be such a delight, with the sharp tang of fall in the air making everything seem crisper and fresher. However, riders need to keep a careful watch on weather changes and pay attention to all forecasts, as it is quite possible to get caught in heavy snowfalls and have to lay over for a few days.

It is possible to tour almost anywhere in the country during many of the off-season months, particularly March, April, early May, late September, October and even into November. Obviously, you will have to watch weather conditions pretty closely (with icy roads being a possible danger in several areas), but the scenery can be quite beautiful at these times, especially in the fall. Added to which, there are fewer crowds; tourist spots are relatively empty and accommodations are much easier to obtain.

Touring in the spring offers the big advantage of getting you outdoors after a winter spent cooped up inside. It also happens to be a great time to go fishing, which may be why I particularly enjoy getting away on a tour at this time of the year.

But let's go back to planning our 16-day tour and, on this occasion, let's assume it's summer—so we'll have no need to consider weather restrictions. If you have any special interests, such as hiking, fishing or visiting places of historical interest, this will help narrow down your selection and give you some idea of the areas worth considering. It is also useful to keep a file for any information on places of particular interest to you, so that you can refer to it at times like these. Most of this information will come from magazine articles that you read during the year and, if they happen to be in a publication that you do not wish to cut up, you will need to place a 3 x 5-inch card in your file with details of the issue date, page and so on, in order that you can refer back to it when you need to. It is also worth noting down the names of anyone who tells you about places of interest, so you can contact them if you need more details when you eventually decide to go.

If you have nowhere definite in mind and just want a pleasant tour, you will need to know how to select the most interesting roads—after all, they tend to look much the same on paper, unless you are particularly good at reading your map. I usually favor roads that follow water, since these are often among the oldest and most historic in the country. I particularly enjoy river roads, although there are also many pretty routes along the shoreline of the larger lakes, a bay, or even the ocean. Most of these roads began as game trails. They were used by Indians for centuries and finally adopted by settlers of this country, who transformed them first into footpaths and then into wagon tracks. Later they became dirt roads and, finally, developed into today's paved highways. Campgrounds are fairly abundant along these routes and, with water nearby, there are often facilities for fishing and swimming.

My second choice of roads are those that wind their way through hills and mountains. They usually make great motorcycle routes, with plenty of curves and ups and downs. They often pass through towns and, once the road has climbed for awhile, you are certain to be treated to some spectacular views. This sort of terrain is generally characterized by huge expanses of national forest, usually indicated on a map by green shading. Here we will find much of general interest and, once again, a good choice of campsites.

I am not a great lover of tourist spots, but there are three places in the United States that I consider well worth visiting by any touring rider. They are the Grand Canyon, Washington, D.C. and Yellowstone National Park. Midwesterners are best positioned for making reasonably short trips to all three. Anyone else will almost certainly have to make a long tour out to at least one of them.

Certainly a trip to Washington, D.C. should not be rushed, as there are so many places you should not miss under any circumstances. It is also preferable to allow time for a short swing to the South as you approach this part of the country, in order to start off with a visit to Colonial Williamsburg and Jamestown, Virginia, the site of our first representative government, along with a string of other firsts for government and our country.

Ride on to Washington, D.C. and absorb some of the magnificence of the nation's capital. Be sure to visit the Lincoln and Washington monuments, as well as the Smithsonian Institution. You might like to follow this with a run up to Gettysburg for a look at the famous Civil War battlefield there, and then ride over to Philadelphia for a look at the Liberty Bell and Independence Hall. It all adds up to a real American history tour, one which will take you a very minimum of seven days, and, even then, you will only have savored a small taste of it.

The area of tidewater Virginia and Maryland is a delightful touring location on its own, and you are sure to regret not being able to spend more time in this area.

Riders living in the East have a much easier time getting to all these places of interest; they can make weekend and day trips and familiarize themselves with much of this fascinating area. For them, the big trips will be to the western states, to see the other two major attractions mentioned—the Grand Canyon and Yellowstone National Park.

Here again, it is unlikely that these will be the only places included in the tour. Most riders will want to take a run up the Pacific Coast, at least the section through California, so they can really feel they have been to the West.

Most of the major places of interest can be covered in a seven- or eight-day visit, excluding the time taken to get to the starting point which, in this example, we will make the Grand Canyon. This spectacular area is worth a day on its own, if only so you do not miss one of the magnificent sunsets or sunrises for which it is famous.

Next, head for Las Vegas, before swinging on over to Los Angeles, or even down to San Diego and a short visit to Tijuana, Mexico. Ride up the coast on US-101 and Highway 1 to San Francisco, before heading back east with a stop in Salt Lake City and on up to Yellowstone National Park.

If all these places are visited, even briefly, we are talking about a fairly hectic schedule and not much short of 350 miles a day for seven long days. Either of these tours would make a great vacation for almost any rider, but they would be strenuous and quite demanding physically if done at the pace described. Still, it would undoubtedly be a trip to be remembered for many years.

I would not suggest tackling such an intense tour until several other trips have been made that have included long days on the road. If you are not completely confident in your ability to cope with such a demanding schedule—and get some enjoyment from it—I would recommend that you add a few more days and travel at a more leisurely pace.

It often helps reduce the risk of extreme fatigue on travel days if you rely on motel stops, rather than attempting to camp. This also makes it easier to set off early in the day and keep riding until late. Once you reach your selected area, you can slow your pace and start using campgrounds. This slower pace also allows much traveling along back roads, at low speed, stopping early and starting late in the morning whenever it suits you.

It should be fairly obvious by now that there are some traps to be avoided when selecting an area for a tour. If your daily mileage aims are too demanding, you risk ruining your enjoyment of the whole trip. Constantly remind yourself that it is not enough to simply ride through an area; to tour takes time and a little effort.

It can be very satisfying to really get to know an area in which you've toured. When someone asks about it, you will be able to recall exactly what it is like, how the people live, what food they like, how it was established and what kind of people live there now. You will be able to picture its cities, towns and villages, its parks, roads and scenery; in other words, you will have truly "been there,"—which in my opinion is what touring is really about.

Chapter 12
Trip Planning

Trip planning can be lots of fun, even when you are not really expecting to go anywhere for a while.

However, for the purposes of this chapter, we are going to assume you already have a date and a destination for your next tour. You have selected an area that looks interesting; it is a reasonable ride away, a near perfect distance for the time you have allowed; you have heard about several really interesting attractions in the locality; and, besides, the roads just look tempting on the map.

Now the real planning starts—but to do it properly, you will require certain information. Basically, you need to get hold of as much detail about the area as you can, then select which of it will be of use to you while on the road.

Your trip will benefit from two types of planning: long range and short range. The first is done weeks, even months, before you leave and covers the entire trip. The second takes place while you are away and deals with just a day or two at a time. It is important that your long range planning should not be too detailed, since it is very easy to set too rigid a schedule. Schedules are fine for airlines, trains and so on, but they are not necessary on a motorcycle tour. By schedule, I am referring to an itinerary that calls for dates, times and places. My "plan" simply lists places worth visiting and activities that I might like to include.

I find it adds to the enjoyment of touring if plans are kept deliberately vague. I have no wish to know exactly where I will be going on any one tour, and I positively resent knowing where I will be, or should be, at any given time. This does not mean that the whole tour is done aimlessly. It just means that I will respond to however I am feeling at the time. If it seems as though the day should be spent lying beneath a tree watching the grass grow, then that is exactly the sort of day I expect it to be!

If I were to write it down, one of my normal touring schedules would read something like this:

Days 1- 4—Ride from California to Kentucky
Days 5-12—Tour Kentucky
Days 13-17—Ride from Kentucky to California

In other words, I know I am going to Kentucky, so I can accumulate all the information I am likely to need on that state. I will also study the map, so I will have some idea of the routes I will use on the outward and homeward journeys, but even that may well change mid-tour.

Let us now consider the best ways to get the information needed on any given area. Ideally, you want to go directly to the state or states you wish to cover, with a polite letter to the relevant Department of Tourism—which will almost always reward you with a big packet of leaflets and brochures. This will usually include a road map of the state, plus some flowery descriptions of the various attractions it offers.

If your chosen area covers more than one state—it may well extend into parts of several states—you will probably want to write each different department for their tourist information packet. (The mailing addresses are obtainable from your public library.)

Another excellent source of information is the AAA auto club. It publishes a series of tour books available to members, which would be a real asset to your travel planning.

Road atlases are also useful at this stage, but you will need to remember or copy down the information, since they are usually too bulky to be worth taking on a motorcycle. I favor the 11 x 15-inch road atlas for home use. You will probably already have used it to select your touring area. Now it will provide you with details of routes and possible side trips or places of interest.

You will also need an oil company map for each of the areas selected for touring, which will supply a lot of extra information. I tend to favor the maps produced by Texaco, which can be obtained from one of its travel service offices at 312 South Michigan Avenue, Chicago, Illinois 60604; or 135 East 42nd Street, New York, New York 10017.

Texaco maps are particularly useful as they mark the most scenic routes with a line of dashes beside the specified road. They also show most public campgrounds, including state and federal parks and recreation areas and the parks are listed separately with a note about the facilities and activities available. Many places of interest will also be marked on the maps, including museums, forts, restorations and historical sites.

The great advantage of having lots of information about your chosen touring area is that you are almost certain to come across extra places worth visiting that you might easily have missed otherwise.

For instance, a trip to Arizona will almost certainly include the Grand Canyon, but, having read enough about the state, you will probably find there are other places in the locality that hold very nearly equal appeal. These will be added to your "must see" list. In this example, one of these additions might be the Petrified Forest National Park, which is well worth a visit. There are also likely to be some places that sound interesting, but which you would be prepared to skip if you ran out of time or found another place that looked as though it might be better.

I show my order of priorities on the map by using two or three pens of different color—preferably the type intended for map-marking that will not obliterate what is underneath. I use one color for the "must see" places. Here there is no particular limit on numbers, but it usually works out to only about three or four in each state or geological area. Each tour will be planned around these selected locations, so I can be almost certain I will visit all of them. There is no order or time allocation just yet; that will normally be considered in my short-range plan.

Next, I mark all the slightly less important places, using a different color. This section often includes some great roads I have heard about or ridden before and wish to revisit.

The final group, marked in a third color, are places I will visit if I get the chance, but will make no real effort to include. Since you are likely to mark far more on your map than you could possibly hope to see in one trip, it is unlikely you will have time for many of these. They can, however, prove useful as extras—places you might visit if they happen to be near an overnight stop, when you would not have time to get to one of your higher priority sites. You might also decide to include one of these with a meal stop. They just seem to be handy to know about when you are in the area.

It is a good idea to make a note of any indoor options, such as museums, caves or historical monuments, which you might like to consider if the weather turns against you. This can be indicated on your map, or you may prefer to list them in a notebook kept with it.

Another useful move is to mark your map for a much larger area than you intend to cover on a given visit. This allows you to alter your route more easily at any time, taking in, say, the northern section rather than the south and leaving the rest for your next trip to the area. In this case, you will also be able to gather additional information during your first visit, which you can browse through on your return home and make use of next time out.

Once your map is marked up, it can be tucked away safely until you reach your touring area. All you need now are final details of possible routes there and back, and your long-range planning is complete—no detailed schedules, no fixed routes and no timetables—just a relaxed, flexible touring program.

When you are working out your routes and touring outline, it is important to look closely at any high elevation areas through which you may be traveling. For example, most visitors are unaware that the south rim of the Grand Canyon is around 7,000 feet, while the north rim is almost 8,000 feet. This may not be too important for a quick stop on a summer's afternoon, but the camper or rider who hits the area in the off-season may well be caught in unexpectedly cold conditions, for which he is not properly prepared. This could easily ruin your visit.

It does not take a great deal of effort to guard against such happenings. If you study your map carefully and rely on the information available, you should get a good idea whether you need to take extra clothing or gear with you. It could be as simple as adding an extra sweater or pair of wool socks—but it could make all the difference.

It can also be very satisfying to be able to pass on this type of information. I remember one such occasion when I was standing at the south rim of the Grand Canyon. An Easterner got out of his car beside me and commented, "Boy, that wind is really

*Tour planning is not only practical,
it adds to the fun of anticipation,
and by making more efficient use
of the time available, allows
the riders to see and do
more while on the tour.*

cold!" which enabled me to respond knowledgeably, "Yeah, it's about 7,000 feet here!" He looked suitably impressed and it led to a conversation about my bike and motorcycle touring in general. I may not have entirely converted him, but it gave him something to think about for sure.

It is just as well to start your long-range planning well ahead of your trip since it takes time to accumulate all the information you need. This particularly applies if you wish to research any of the area's special attributes that interest you. For instance, if you are heading into Indian country, it could be an advantage to know something of the background of the tribe or tribes that live there. You may even be able to find a book on the historical events relating to the area. If your interests lie in other directions, such as in fishing, hiking or spelunking, you should be able to get a good idea of what the area has to offer in that respect.

Short-range planning cannot really be started until your trip is underway and then it can only be done for one or two days at a time. Once you are in your selected area, you can take out your marked-up map and decide what to do the following day. Be prepared to change your mind, though—or have it changed for you—so you can make the most of any opportunities that come your way.

For instance, you may allow yourself an hour to look around a museum that is on your tour, but once there, meet an old-timer who has some fascinating tales to tell about life in the area many years ago. It would make no sense to leave in a hurry just to stick to your program, since a talk like this could make your whole trip, perhaps putting you on to some really out-of-the-way places that you would not wish to miss. So make the most of any unexpected turn of events, if it is favorable.

If your plans are sufficiently flexible, there should be no problem in altering them slightly or even completely discarding them—and that is the ideal situation.

So be sure to keep all plans indefinite, whether long or short term, and accept the unexpected when it comes along. The best way to prepare for your tour is just to acquire the knowledge you need about your selected area, not to give yourself a rigid schedule to abide by. By knowing what is available, you will be able to tailor your travels to your interests and can pick and choose what you want to see as you go along.

It really does not matter if you cannot see everything. With your map as a guide, you will be able to visit all your priority places, and, after all, if you go everywhere of interest the first time around, you will not have nearly such a good excuse to return some day.

Chapter 13
The Money Angle

Motorcycle touring is not the poor man's sport it was once believed to be, so it is inevitable that most of us will have to look carefully at the costs involved. Fortunately, it is still possible to manage on a fairly tight budget, but you need to know what you are doing and where the best spending cuts can be made.

Your bank balance, or lack of one, will dictate much of your approach to touring, particularly influencing the bike you select, the amount and type of accessories, your clothing system, as well as where you travel and how often you can get away. Most of us suffer from a lack of readily available cash, especially at the start when we still have everything to buy. The answer is simple. If you cannot afford all you need right away, pick out the essentials and be prepared to make compromises. For example, if the bike you want is slightly more than you were expecting to pay, forget about the saddlebags and a fairing for the time being, or accept re-thinking your choice of machine.

There are two major areas of spending that need to be looked at closely if you are on a limited touring budget. Your first and biggest expenses will obviously be the bike, accessories and all the touring equipment; these are usually one-time purchases, so in general you can forget about them once they are made. However, you should not ignore the second area which covers the actual cost of touring and, as a recurring expense, is as important as the first. There is no point in owning your dream touring machine if you cannot afford to go anywhere on it!

In theory at least, it should be possible in both these areas to keep costs down to whatever you can afford, but in practice you are likely to be tempted to go over your original budget. Be prepared to drop certain nonessential purchases if this happens. It is undoubtedly very easy to spend a considerable amount of money if you want top quality equipment and luxury items, but it is equally possible to get by on basic items and still tour comfortably. Obviously there is a minimum amount you will have to be prepared to pay and we will be looking at approximate figures a little later in this chapter. The total figure for equipping yourself to go motorcycle touring will be greatly reduced if you already own a suitable machine. If it is not already equipped for touring, you will have to expect a fair amount of expense here.

If you are starting out without a bike, or with one totally unsuited to touring, you have the difficult and expensive task of selecting the right machine. If you simply cannot afford the new model you want, you might consider a used bike. This can make a lot of sense, particularly if you are fairly new to motorcycling and are likely to want to change your machine within a short time. It is quite possible to find a full dress touring machine in excellent condition, with low mileage and only one owner, at quite a reasonable price. This is partly because accessories depreciate much faster than motorcycles.

For example, a new motorcycle will depreciate about 20% the first year and 10% per year for the next two or three, depending on its condition, mileage and the price increases of new models. On the other hand, major accessories, such as fairings and saddlebags, depreciate by about 50% the first year and 10% for the next two or three. It is fairly obvious that a one- or two-year-old machine that has been fully equipped and well-loved can be a very good deal.

There are disadvantages to buying second-hand, of course. You would be extremely lucky to find the exact combination of bike and accessories that you want, so you must be prepared to accept whatever is available. Financing will be more difficult than with a new model and you will only qualify for a two-year loan, as opposed to the three years normally offered on a new machine. It is much better if you have saved enough cash, for you will be in a stronger bargaining position when the right machine becomes available.

I have always preferred to save a little longer and buy a new bike. This has the advantage of allowing you to select the exact model you want, in the right color and with the right accessories. You can also shop around to get the best price. There is much to be said for buying your bike and major accessories from the same dealer, especially if they are to be financed. It gives the dealer more latitude in overall cost and, in addition, it means only one place to return to for any maintenance or warranty work.

Your next major financial consideration will be your riding clothes. All too often this is given low priority and riders will settle for a mix-match of whatever they already own, perhaps left over from some other outdoor sport that will "do for the time being."

My view is that this category is too important to be neglected. At least a part of the bike accessories budget should be set aside for proper riding attire. At the very least this means a suitable helmet, leather jacket, two pairs of gloves, decent boots and rainsuit.

Let us now make some rough calculations of overall costs, at least for these initial purchases. First, we can estimate the cost of the new bike as follows:

                    1000cc and over — $3,900-$4,300
                    750cc to 950cc — $3,200-$3,600
                    500cc to 700cc — $2,300-$2,700
                      under 500cc — $1,700-$2,100

We can add about 10% to 20% for accessories, depending upon personal requirements. All these prices are very much dependent upon inflation and the changing value of the dollar, since so much of the equipment comes from abroad, especially from Japan and Germany.

One other type of bike not yet included in our price list is the factory-equipped touring machine. This will cost from around $5,500 to $7,700 and, of course, you will not need additional accessories for it.

Clothing is the next big item on the touring budget and, as we have already discussed, it is an important part of your spending. If you are traveling two-up, this will involve double the amount of expense, but even so it is *not* a good area in which to try to cut costs. You should at least equip yourself with a good helmet, riding suit and so on, as already suggested. It often proves to be a false saving if you go for the cheapest clothing you can find, since it gets such hard use that it will quickly need replacing. Since your safety is also involved here, it makes no sense to make do with inferior goods.

The subject of suitable clothing was discussed in depth in Chapter 5, so we will just talk about costs here. As a very rough guide, you can allow about 10% of the bike's price to clothe each of the riders. Even if it means reducing the size of the down payment, or sacrificing some of the accessories, it is wise to get the right clothing.

Before long you will need to consider completing your clothing system with items suitable for bad weather. Obviously you will have to wait until your finances have recovered from the shock of those initial purchases, but you will not regret what you spend on quality riding gear. It is amazing how a really cold ride can make the proper clothing seem reasonably priced!

Next you will probably want to look at soft luggage, in particular a good tank bag and possibly a duffle bag. You will need these at about the same time you buy your camping gear, if you decide to go that route.

There is no need to rush out and buy all your camping gear at once, since you can manage for quite a while on very little equipment. Your tent, sleeping bag and mattress will represent the largest savings in travel costs, so they should be given priority in your budget.

Your final major group of expenses will once again focus on your motorcycle. Once you have done a little traveling with your newly equipped bike, you will almost certainly find areas you want to improve. If you are lucky, this will mean just a few dollars for a forgotten item or two, but it could easily be the need for new rear suspension parts or a custom seat which could cost several hundred dollars.

While there are some substantial costs involved in getting started, these can be spread over a lengthy period thanks to financing and planned purchases. If your touring motorcycle can also double as your regular form of transportation, it may be easier to justify the expense. In any case, it represents a fair resale value, either as a trade-in on another machine or as an outright sale.

Let us now look at some approximate maximum and minimum costs involved in motorcycle touring, if a rider is starting from scratch. About the very least you will need is $2,000, and it is easy enough to spend over $10,000 if you insist on having the

In general, the least expensive accommodations are the older, out-of-the-way motels, with prices increasing for newer buildings and more convenient locations near expressways or larger towns and cities. Expect to find the highest prices in downtown hotels or resort areas.

$12 - 15
Rural and small towns

$16 - 24
Next to major highways and near cities

best of everything and are not particularly concerned about money. We are therefore looking at an average of about $6,000 for the initial expenditure on the touring motorcycle, basic accessories, clothing and equipment. It seems a lot compared with prices just five or 10 years ago, but we should remember that there is a great deal more choice and quality today. The higher costs are not just a reflection of inflation; they also represent some major advances in materials and designs.

Travel costs are fairly easy to predict, since they are closely related to the rest of the economy. Your major expenses will be fuel, food and overnight accommodations, and it is possible to make an accurate calculation of what these will be, providing you know where you are heading and whether you will be camping, using motels or both.

Fuel costs will depend upon the miles you travel and the mpg of your motorcycle (if you are not sure of it, base your calculations on 40 mpg). You can use the price of gas in your area, plus about 10%, to get a fairly accurate figure. Our calculations will look something like the following:

Gas selling at $1.35 -
Cost per 1,000 miles = 1,000 + 40 × (1.35 + .135)
                     = 37.125

If we round this off to $40 per 1,000 miles, it will cover any oil or chain lube that we need. From this we can see that a 5,000-mile trip will cost about $200. You may also need to add the cost of a new tire, which would mean an additional $35 to $70, plus service charge unless you do the job yourself. I usually keep a $100 emergency fund for any trip over 1,000 miles, so a new tire would come out of this with no problem.

Any other road expenses should be minimal—unless you get a traffic violation. You may be required to pay on the spot, and it is possible that a personal check may not be acceptable to a court.

Tolls are not generally more than a couple of dollars at a time, but there are places in the East where they occur so frequently that they can quickly mount up (fortunately there are few tolls in the West). For instance, getting in and out of New York City can be quite an expensive business, and there is a fairly high toll at the Chesapeake Bay Bridge-Tunnel.

It can be fun to use ferries at some time during your travels. They will often save you time and a lot of frustration, but you should remember to include them in your budgeting since they can be quite costly—perhaps even a major expense on your trip. I am thinking in particular of the Alaskan ferry down to Prince Rupert and the Canadian ferry from Prince Rupert to Vancouver Island. However, it is easy enough to find out these costs in advance so they do not take you by surprise.

At present, both Canadian and Mexican fuel costs are below U.S. costs, so you should stay well within your budget, at least that part of it, if you are planning to tour in those countries.

Camping is the most economical form of overnight stop, and it is also the easiest for which to budget since the costs of campgrounds vary only slightly from state to state. In Chapter 8, we suggested that $4 per night would be about average, and this would be a reasonably accurate figure to use, particularly on a long trip. This allows for stops in some of the more expensive private campgrounds, which will cost between $6 to $8 a night, as well as using the primitive Forest Service sites which usually cost $2 or less and, more often than not, are free. State and federal park campsites will run close to the $4 a night rate and that usually covers both solo and two-up riders.

Most campers will be able to manage easily on about $5 per person daily for food. A couple spending three or more days in one place will probably be able to halve that amount. If you are really short of cash, it would even be possible to cut food bills to $2 a day. Obviously, all these figures will depend considerably on your normal choice of foods and the quantity you eat, so you should adjust your budget accordingly. If you can afford it, you have the choice of eating in restaurants all the time and staying in motels or hotels every night. Some will want to go this route the whole time, while most riders will probably like to include this into their tour at some point; some nights in a motel and a few restaurant meals can make a pleasant change after days of camping out and cooking over an open fire.

My normal day on the road starts fairly early (from a motel or a campsite), and I will ride for three or four hours before stopping for breakfast. Usually this coincides with a need for fuel and by this time the temperature has risen sufficiently to require a reduction in clothing. After this, meals will depend upon circumstances and finances.

For instance, if I were in the South during the fall, I would probably look for a fruit stand around midday and have roasted peanuts and freshly picked peaches for lunch. However, if finances allow, I may choose a more substantial lunch in an attractive restaurant or coffee shop. Dinner varies as much as lunch, but it will usually be eaten after I have finished riding at the end of the day, regardless of whether or not I am camping.

Most riders will be able to find motels and restaurants that suit both their pocket and taste, but these are a little difficult to estimate for budget purposes since they vary so much depending upon location, time of the year and sometimes even time of the day. It should be possible to survive on around $6 a day per person for food, even without doing any of your own cooking. It means watching all food costs fairly carefully, whether in a restaurant or supermarket and sometimes settling for sandwiches in a parking lot, or preferably a park, rather than a hot meal.

Perhaps a more realistic daily average would be $10 to $15 per person. This would allow for up to three meals in restaurants. This would still necessitate keeping an eye on costs and choosing the cheaper meals on occasion, but it does not place many restrictions on you.

Few riders will want to settle for exactly the same eating routine day in and day out, so you should allow a little extra in your food budget for those occasional dinners in a special restaurant or a night out at a dinner show in Las Vegas, Reno or South Lake Tahoe. That special dinner could easily cost $12 to $20 per person, excluding the tip and having to make do with domestic wine, while the dinner show could cost at least $30 per person, without drinks.

If you are very conscientious, it is possible to live quite economically even when staying in motels every night. It requires quite a lot of planning, since you must avoid being in or near major cities overnight where prices will be high. You must also stop fairly early to get rooms in the least expensive motels, as they tend to fill up first. In this way, it would be possible for a solo rider to get by on around $12 to $14 a night; a couple on perhaps two dollars more. If two beds are required, add another couple of dollars.

Few of us are willing to go to extremes all the time to keep costs down, but if you are prepared to make some effort to watch expenses, a couple should be able to find a reasonable motel in one of the small towns for $14 to $18 a night, or $16 to $24 in or near the larger cities or close to major highways.

Big hotels in major cities are likely to cost around $40 to $60 minimum. This is certainly true if you want a decent hotel room in Las Vegas or Reno, but motels farther out in the same cities drop to around $20 to $25 a night. Most of the hotel rooms in the French Quarter in New Orleans start at around $40, but you might think it worthwhile since it places everything you are likely to want to see within easy walking distance.

For my own calculations, I usually estimate motel costs at $20 a night solo and $25 two-up. I double these figures if a big city or major resort is on the itinerary. This tends to be slightly on the high side, but it helps my peace of mind and makes it easier to cope when unexpected expenses crop up.

It is not a good idea to carry too much cash with you on a motorcycle, so the obvious answer is to rely on credit cards. I always carry cards from two major oil companies, as well as one or two bank cards. Even if you do not use them for normal expenses, they can be very useful on a long tour in case of breakdowns or other emergencies.

Almost all your fuel costs can go on one or another of the oil company cards, while your hotel or motel costs can be put on one of the bank cards. This greatly reduces the amount of cash you need to carry with you. You can also use your bank cards for a few of the restaurant meals, but most of them and any grocery shopping will have to be paid for in cash. You will also need cash if you are intending to use campgrounds.

I will carry cash, providing the amount is not over $500. If I think I will need more than that, I have the rest in traveler's checks. I always divide any cash between two pockets and my tank bag to minimize the risk of losing the whole amount. On a long tour, one of more than a week, I will usually carry my checkbook. Then if I become really desperate for cash, I allow a day's stop and find a bank that will make a transfer of funds from my account. This usually costs the price of a telephone call and the fee for the transfer through the Federal Reserve system, but it will nearly always be accomplished in one day.

So what should the average touring rider or couple expect to have to pay overall for a week or two away exploring the country? We can figure on a daily average of about $11 for the solo rider who camps and eats one meal a day in a restaurant, preferably breakfast since it is usually the least expensive meal you can buy. A couple living the same way should figure on around $15 a day. If we add about $10 per day to these figures, it will allow for the occasional stay in a motel and the extra meal or two in a better restaurant. We can therefore work on a weekly figure of $147 for the solo rider and $175 for a couple. I consider this a perfectly acceptable way to tour for anyone who, like me, has to watch what he spends in order to enjoy the maximum number of trips, but who does not wish to have to think about money throughout the whole tour.

Using these figures, we end up with a total of $374 spent by the solo rider on a two-week tour covering about 2,000 miles, or $430 for a couple—a pretty good value in anybody's book!

Chapter 14
Equipment Care

Maintenance starts at home, continues while you are on the road and then starts all over again when you get back from your tour. There really seems to be no end to it. Yet, if you want to be sure of relatively trouble-free touring, there is no alternative; it has to be done.

Some of the bikes coming on the market are incorporating many features that reduce, or even eliminate, much of the periodic maintenance, making it all too easy to form bad habits and forget to do any maintenance at all. High mileage touring riders need to be particularly conscientious since this type of use makes regular maintenance essential.

If your motorcycle has a drive chain, this will need a lot of attention. It must be kept well lubricated, and it is best to do this when the chain is warm. It is worth getting into the habit of lubricating it immediately after stopping for gas or meals, a couple of times during the day. Prolonged high speeds are particularly hard on chains, as they are on tires, so if you are riding fast, check the tension of your chain more frequently than normal.

You can forget all about this type of maintenance, however, if your bike is shaft driven. Nor is there any maintenance required for the new style wheels, such as the cast alloy type regularly used these days, or the Comstar wheels used by Honda. The most attention they require is an occasional cleaning and general inspection. Wire-spoked wheels, on the other hand, can sometimes get out of alignment and cause problems. This is particularly likely to occur to the rear wheel of a heavily loaded two-up machine.

When realigning a spoked wheel, the main object is to get the wheel perfectly straight, both laterally and radially. Alignment is easy to check if you can get the wheel turning freely while off the ground (using the center stand is fine if you have one). Place a screwdriver, or something similar, on a box or stand beside the wheel to create a stationary point. With the tip of the screwdriver as close to the wheel as possible without touching (approximately 1/16"), turn the wheel at a reasonable speed (it can be driven by hand) and it should be obvious whether the space between them remains constant. The wheel should not deviate from this point throughout one revolution.

Lateral run-out is any misalignment that shows up in side-to-side movement, whereas radial run-out is any deviation in the wheel from perfect roundness. I check the latter by carefully tightening each spoke until I can tap each one with the end of the wrench and get a musical tone, rather than a thud. I then continue around the wheel, tightening, loosening and tapping, until eventually all the spokes sound the same.

As a final step, the wheel is checked laterally and radially. Usually if the spokes are right, the wheel will be true, but, if not, mark where it is off and go back to adjusting spoke tension.

While putting the wheel back in shape, you have an ideal opportunity to thoroughly inspect the wheel for damage. I have had an alloy, wire-spoked wheel crack under heavy loads while touring. They were only stress fractures when they were noticed, but they would almost certainly have resulted in worse problems had they not been detected in time.

This brings me to a really important point. Just by examining your machine periodically, it is amazing how many potential problems can be detected before they develop into something serious. There are two ideal opportunities for accomplishing this on a regular basis. The first is while you are washing and waxing your motorcycle. You will be looking at it closely anyway, so it makes sense to keep an eye open for anything that might be wearing out or coming loose. The second chance you get is at nut and bolt tightening time. This should take place at least weekly when you are on the road and, at the same time, you can give the machine an overall visual inspection. Any oil leaks? How are the brake fluid levels, if your bike has disc brakes? What about the wear indicators on the brakes? At the same time, check such items as the clutch and brake cables in case adjustment is necessary.

It is worth keeping a record of the maintenance you do on your machine. If nothing else, it serves as a reminder that it needs to be done. If your bike has wire-spoked wheels, it is advisable to check the spoke tension as part of your regular maintenance.

You will be able to manage with the stock tool kit for most of your maintenance work, with perhaps the addition of a six-inch adjustable wrench. I always carry this in the fairing pocket or in the tank bag. In addition I usually take a screwdriver—one that has a removable shaft with a blade tip on one end and a Phillips head on the other. It duplicates the one in the tool kit, but it is easier to get at when the bike is loaded. It is often useful to have two wrenches with you, especially when you need one on each end of a bolt. Since the additional wrench is adjustable, it will fit American-size nuts and bolts, as well as those in metric sizes.

Try to keep your repair kit small, unless your bike has proved it needs a more elaborate one. It can be useful to have some plastic electrician's tape and a few feet of soft wire. It is also worth carrying some spare bulbs and fuses; not having them is the sort of thing that can leave you stranded out on a lonely, dark stretch of road.

One final important part of your bike maintenance is the inspection and measurement of the tread depth of your tires, particularly the rear tire. You can buy a tread

While on a trip, try to avoid routine maintenance chores that could have been handled before departure. Reliability of any bike depends on good maintenance.

depth gauge for about a dollar in auto parts stores and, along with your air pressure gauge, it will enable you to keep a regular check on the state of your tires.

When you buy new tires, or a new bike, record the tread depth in the logbook, along with the odometer reading. After every 500 miles, take a tread depth reading at about five places on the rear tire and record the lowest. You should measure the tread at the very center of the tire. Most tread depth gauges read in 32nds of an inch and most new tires will show 7 to 9/32nds of tread depth.

Tread wear depends on many different factors, including riding style, speed, load, outside temperatures and type of road. By keeping a 500-mile check on your rear tire, you should be able to establish your typical rate of tread wear. I find riding in high temperatures, as in the desert, and long distances at high speeds, result in the greatest amount of tread wear. By keeping a regular check on tread depth, you will greatly minimize the chance of having a blowout or flat tire, since most of these occur when the tread depth gets low, say under 2/32nds. I generally think about fitting a new tire just before the tread depth reaches this level. Since you will know when your tire is ready to be replaced, you will be able to find a dealer in plenty of time and will not be riding on badly worn tires. The front tire has less tread depth initially but wears much more slowly, so that, in general, a rider will go through about two rear tires to each front tire.

Air pressure is as important as the tread depth, but this should be checked when the tire is cold. This means checking it in the morning before starting out or after a meal stop when the tires have had time to cool off. You will find suggested air pressures for your machine in the owner's manual, as well as on the stickers on most new bikes. A higher figure is usually given for high speed and/or loaded conditions, and it is worth paying attention to these. High internal temperatures are the main cause of excessive tread wear and, if the air pressure is too low, the side walls flex more and generate excess heat. You should be able to tell when the air pressure in the tires is correct, since the bike will feel much better. If there is too much air pressure, the bike will ride rather hard, whereas with too little it will feel "mushy" and will be difficult to control precisely.

While checking air pressure and tread depth, take the opportunity to visually inspect the rest of the tire. Check for any type of irregularity, cuts, sidewall damage or anything protruding from the tread. Cast alloy wheels have enabled the use of tubeless tires on motorcycles which essentially eliminates the risk of a blowout, since this is the result of a ruptured tube. Even so, it is worth checking your tires regularly, as major damage can still result in a rapid loss of air which has much the same effect as a blowout, while being a less common occurrence.

If you find you are getting exceptionally good mileage from your tires, such as 7,000 or 8,000 miles from the rear, you might be able to extend the tread depth check interval to every 1,000 miles.

Bike maintenance demands the most attention, but other parts of your touring setup will also need to be looked at from time to time. Your riding clothes will benefit from proper care; not only will they last longer, but they will also function better. Smooth leather is quite easy to look after, which is why I prefer it to suede or rough-out leathers for motorcycling. Rough-textured leathers almost always require dry-cleaning, which can sometimes cost nearly as much as the garment did in the first place. Smooth leather can be cleaned yourself, using just saddlesoap or one of the commercial cleaner/preservatives. This applies to boots, leather jackets, pants, chaps or gloves—all should be cleaned with a soft cloth and saddlesoap. Normally, this would be done at home, but on trips of a month or more, I will often buy a small tin of saddlesoap and clean my leathers while on the road.

I would not recommend any other care for leather, apart from a little wax on the metal zippers to keep them working smoothly. The only leather I consider waterproofing is the foot section of boots. I use mink oil applied with an old toothbrush where the upper meets the sole and a rag on the rest of the foot section. The problem I find with waterproofing is that the breathing qualities of the leather are lost, making it much hotter in warm weather and only slightly warmer in cold weather. I prefer to wear a lightweight waterproof garment over leather clothing, which keeps out the rain while adding warmth.

Since your helmet is important to your safety, it is worth keeping in good condition. It should be visually inspected regularly for any surface cracks or damage to the outer shell. Watch for frayed straps or damaged inner parts. Helmets can be cleaned using soap and water, a sponge and a soft cloth.

Riding suits and other cloth garments can usually be machine washed, but follow the instructions on the garments. After washing a riding suit, I spray it with Scotchgard to improve water repellency. I also do this when the garment is brand new and still store-clean. It is worth giving this treatment to any cloth items that are going to be exposed to the weather, such as tank bags and duffle bags. Many rainsuits will require seam-sealing, and there are products available for this, appropriately called "seam sealers." Look for them in sporting goods stores where hiking and backpacking gear is sold. Alternatively, you may find them in yachting stores where, incidentally, you can sometimes find good rain gear suitable for motorcycling.

It is worth taking a small tube of seam sealant with you when you tour, but be sure to keep it in a plastic bag in case it leaks. It is quite good for small leaks in your tent as well as in your rain gear.

Most maintenance of camping gear is done at home and, on the whole, it is simply a matter of cleaning and inspecting it. Your tent should not have been put away wet or dirty, but if it was, be sure to check it over for damage. In any case, it is worth opening it up and inspecting it before you leave. Sleeping bags should be aired before you set out, and once on the road, try to hang them in the sun whenever you get the chance, as it will keep them dry and sweet-smelling.

Once back home, store them loosely out of their stuff bags. If you buy your sleeping bag without a storage bag, you can make one simply enough—a good-sized (three feet by four feet), light cotton sack is all you need. Unroll foam sleeping pads and store them open or loosely rolled if space is a problem; the same applies to air mattresses.

Finally, clean up and check over the rest of your camping gear. Repack it—and you are ready for your next trip.

Chapter 15
Summary

Now that we have looked at a myriad of details about motorcycle touring, I may as well confess that you can actually set off without knowing any of it!

I well recall my first tour, back in the early '50s, when I must have done everything wrong. My motorcycle happened to be the only form of transportation I had, and it represented the cheapest way to make a trip back home to Santa Ana, California, from my base at Fort Worth, Texas.

Was it a good touring bike? I never gave it a thought, although it was probably one of the best available at the time. It was a 1948 hand-shift, hard-tailed, 74-cubic-inch Harley-Davidson.

Accessories? I had bought the machine second-hand, and it had a windshield and leather saddlebags already on it. Oh yes, there was one other accessory—a set of plastic streamers attached to the end of each handlebar. I never quite figured out why they were there, but I left them on. I'm sure they served some vital aerodynamic function!

My riding clothes were not exactly suited to long-distance touring, I must admit. It never really occurred to me that I would need anything other than my regular Levis, engineer boots and T-shirts, plus my leather jacket with all its zippers, snaps and buckles, my leather gloves and sunglasses. However, I made sure I wore my hat—not helmet, hat—that I'd bought from the Harley shop. I thought it looked grand with its itty-bitty visor and gold-colored cord across the top, creating a 50-mission crush, as seen on a World War II fighter pilot's hat. Since it was summertime and I was traveling from one warm climate to another, I assumed I was properly dressed for the occasion. How could I need anything else in 85-degree weather?

This is a classic misconception shared by most riders who have never traveled any real distance. I had been riding that old Harley a lot and fell into the common trap of assuming that riding *frequently* was much the same as riding long distance; the latter imposes a degree of severity that simply is not experienced during regular short journeys.

It is not essential to be ideally dressed for the weather when you are making 30- or 40-minute trips locally; if you are fairly comfortable, it is good enough. However, in the same clothing and the same temperature, you would feel really miserable after an hour or so at sustained speed along the highway—as I soon discovered on that memorable first trip.

My next unpleasant surprise came on the second day when I found it was almost too painful to sit on the bike, let alone ride it. In addition, the grips felt as if they had swelled to twice their normal size, and I had great difficulty holding on to them. I could hardly believe it. I felt sure I had been out on my bike for a complete day before. What I failed to appreciate was the difference between riding around "all day" locally, taking regular lengthy breaks, and sitting in the saddle for 12 to 14 hours with only a few brief stops.

The final blow to my confidence came when the sun went down while I was still crossing the desert. I felt sure I would freeze to death in the 60-degree-or-so temperature that night. It was just as well I did not hit any bad weather!

There's little doubt I was ill-prepared for that 10-day, 4,000-mile tour. I was miserably cold for parts of the trip and took unnecessary chances to get the journey over with as quickly as possible. I also very nearly ran out of money, which meant spending part of one night sleeping next to the gas pumps of a closed service station. Yet, looking back on it, I'm certain I enjoyed the experience.

Recently, I made a trip of twice the distance which started out over much of the route I took on that journey nearly 30 years ago. This time I was on a brand new Honda GL1100 Interstate, with its full set of standard accessories, all checked out and in perfect condition for the trip.

It was early in the year, so I ran into bad weather with temperatures in the teens and rain so heavy that cars were pulling off the roads. Throughout the trip I remained warm, dry and comfortable. I was well-enough equipped to be able to enjoy everything from fishing in Florida to night clubs in the New Orleans French Quarter. It had taken me only an hour or so to get completely packed for the trip and my cost calculations were only about $20 off over the entire three-week trip.

Strangely enough, I find it hard to decide which of these two trips gave me the most pleasure. Without doubt, the first was the greater adventure, introducing me to something totally unknown. The second was as much fun—not quite as exciting—but far more satisfying in that I had been amply equipped for every occasion.

This is partly why I have written this book. It has taken me the best part of 30 years to acquire this knowledge and I see no reason not to share it, since there is no need for anyone to go the entire length of the hard route to motorcycle touring, providing they are receptive to suggestions. I have included information about equipment and touring methods that I have found useful, along with the reasons they worked for me. You can decide their value for yourself.

Even if you follow every tip in this book, you will still find traps to fall into and mistakes to make. It seems strange to me that for years I only knew part of the story—that my knowledge and experiences were incomplete—because at the time, I felt I knew it all. Now I know that I still have a lot to learn. There is a lot of experimenting left for you, me and anyone else who travels the road on a motorcycle. And, if you are setting off for the first time, please be advised that motorcycle riding and touring are addictive. I am just as hooked now as I was when, as a wild-eyed teenager, I crossed the Arizona desert in shirt sleeves and a Harley hat.